M000074088

THE
THEATRE
QUOTATION
BOOK

~

To: Gruff +
Richard

Thought you two should
have this on hand!

Love,
Divtago
Paul
+
Holland
2008

THE
THEATRE
QUOTATION
BOOK

*A Treasury of
Insights and Insults*

collected and edited by
RUSSELL VANDENBROUCKE

Foreword by TONY KUSHNER

LIMELIGHT EDITIONS · New York

First Limelight Edition November 2001

Copyright © 2001 by Russell Vandenbroucke

All rights reserved under International and Pan American Copyright
Conventions. Published in the United States by Proscenium Publishers
Inc., New York.

Interior design by Trudi Gershenov

Drawings copyright © 2001 by Caroline Wallace

Printed in the United States of America

Library of Congress Cataloging-in-Publication Data

The Theatre quotation book : a treasury of insights and insults / collected and edited by Russell Vandenbroucke.
   p. cm.
     Includes index.
     ISBN 0-87910-959-9
     1. Theater--Quotations, maxims, etc. I. Vandenbroucke, Russell.

PN6084.T48 T49 2001
792--dc21

2001029886

For wordsmiths, playwrights, and artisans:
Craftsmen—and women—all

A proverb is the wisdom of many and the wit of one.
ANONYMOUS

True Wit is Nature to advantage dressed,
What oft was thought, but ne'er so well expressed.
ALEXANDER POPE

I often quote myself. It adds spice to my conversation.
GEORGE BERNARD SHAW

Have you ever observed that we pay much more attention to a wise passage when it is quoted than when we
read it in the original author?
PHILIP G. HAMERTON

Two ideas by violence yoked together.
SAMUEL JOHNSON, describing a metaphysical conceit

In this process of compounding, two things added
together do not produce a third thing but suggest some
fundamental relation between them.
HUGH KENNER

A trained mind is needed to relish a non sequitur.
N.F. SIMPSON

Men's maxims reveal their characters.
LUC DE CLAPIERS

Contents

FOREWORD
by Tony Kushner

Herman Melville began *Moby Dick* with pages of quotes about whales. These were compiled, Melville tells us, by a sub-sub-librarian, a pale Bartleby-like creature who lives in a world made entirely of books, who has never set foot out-of-doors much less encountered a living whale on the open seas, but who seems to be trying to conjure up the cetological thing itself by composing it out of hundreds (and ultimately, as we proceed into the novel proper, out of hundreds of thousands) of words. And he succeeds in creating, if not a whale, then something colossal, prodigious, a leviathan.

Melville was a man of the sea, he was famous for having first-hand knowledge of its mysteries and dangers, for not being an armchair traveler, not a sub-sub-librarian. So why does he embark on the sea epic that is *Moby Dick* in the guise of a bookworm? One obvious answer: the seas upon which the Pequod sails and the monster it chases are of the mind and soul, the Pequod more a submarine than a sailing ship, its motion vertical rather than horizontal, its voyage interior, not an exploration of objective life but of the vast subjectivity beneath the roiling surface, a subjectivity built of that selfsame material by means of which it may be pondered and reported: words. The irreducible molecular structure of the world of *Moby Dick* consists of words, sentences, "information," quotes—it's a world made of words, of books. As what world is not?

Russell Vandenbroucke, director, playwright, producer, dramaturg, scholar, all around working man (and true gentleman) of the theater, appears to us here costumed as a sub-sub-librarian, having compiled this delicious florilegium of responsible and irresponsible, mad, maddening and irrefutable observations, opinions and truths about the theater's many component parts. This book is made of many books, the consequence of a lifetime of reading, a lifetime of taking notes, listening, observing, searching for ways of pinning down, or at any rate describing fields of uncertainty around, the Great Ineffable.

It works! A Vandenbrouckian theater is conjured up out of words! To graze at random through the book, your eye snagged by famous names or names unknown to you, is to acquire many useful and handy morsels, words to contemplate and words to offer at cocktail parties. But to read the whole book is to read a little theatrical Kaballah, sequences of densely-packed anecdotes and pronouncements inviting the reader to expand, to open up, to move deeper within.

OK, so a lot of what is recorded here is funny and flip and castoff, and while Hegel and Kant and Aristotle put in their appearances, some of what our hunter and gatherer has offered us seems a little tatty, a little gossamer to be keeping company with Melville, the Kaballah and the Great Ineffable, but isn't that precisely what theater is like? Turn your head this way, it's vulgarity Incarnate; turn your head that way, it's the Great Ineffable, more like Life than Life itself, which has a way (Life itself that is) of being similarly tricky and Janus-faced.

And dialectical: every baldly stated opinion and aperçu immediately provokes an argument, which is the joy of the brief quotation, of the aphorism: As soon as you hear someone say "It is thus!" you must respond "The Hell it is!" unless you're a Moonie. Any assertion should generate its antithesis, and the more elegantly or wittily the assertion is phrased, the more magisterial its tone, the more generative of contradiction it ought to be, because elegance and wit and a good performance stimulate thought, and thought stimulates contradiction. If you read this book in a lively fashion, you will conclude by being deeply confused as to what you think about theater, and that is a very good place to be.

And in conclusion, I would like to disavow everything I'm quoted as having said or written.

PREFACE

Samuel Beckett once explained that what he appreciated about St. Augustine's "Do not despair, one of the thieves was saved; do not presume, one of the thieves was damned" was the symmetry of the sentence rather than its implied theology. Anyone who savors language—through the eye in reading, the ear in hearing, the lips in speaking, or the fingertips in writing—can appreciate the equipoise of Augustine's assertion as much as its sense. Its form appeals as much as its meaning.

I cannot remember the beginning of my own love of language, but I wonder if it began with prayers and nursery rhymes I memorized by rote without understanding their precise meaning. Sheer repetition made them familiar, pleasing, comforting. In addition, my father had a delightful repertoire of playful phrases that he invented. In high school, I began to read the dictionary and planned to finish it the summer I graduated. I started enthusiastically with exotic words under "q," "x," and "z," but delved no further.

In college, I learned to bolster research papers by citing the implicit authority of others. Quotations sometimes strengthened my argument; they always eased the journey toward the requisite five, ten, or twenty pages. By the time I began graduate school I had committed a few of my favorite sentences to memory, eloquent expressions by Beckett, Camus, Faulkner, and Joyce. I did not will myself to learn these. Rather, certain quotations struck my fancy then stuck in my gray matter, at least in paraphrased form.

In drama school, I first encountered Richard Gilman's penchant for quotations marked by beauty and wit as well as insight. I marveled at his repertoire. An entire semester passed before I started hearing his favorites a second time. While hoping one day to write as gracefully as he, a failed aspiration, I decided to preserve the deft expressions I encountered as a means to possess them. Thus began my collection on three-by-five cards. Most came from reading. Some are from stories, perhaps apocryphal, that I was told. A few were uttered spontanteously, unforgettably, during rehearsal breaks and green room chatter.

Three years after I began to collect quotes, my wife gave me a copy of *The Chicago Manual of Style* to guide me in completing a book. Her inscription lovingly skewered at least two of my habits: "For Russ, who always has the last word, but wants to make sure it's the right one." She also gave me the book whose grace, humor, and brevity has been my model, *The Writer's Quotation Book: A Literary Companion*, edited by James Charlton. It immediately became my favorite opening-night present for dozens of playwrights, directors, actors, and designers over the years.

~∂

One of the theatre's eternal pleasures is transporting an audience effortlessly through time and space. Along the way, we encounter revelations that one character makes to another. One of the pleasures in structuring these quotations has been the opportunity to take words uttered centuries and continents apart, then create repartee among people who never met.

Like an actor, I have embraced the borrowed words of another to engage an audience.

"Quoting out of context" is not so much a confession about this collection as its raison d'être. All these words have truth, but none is *the* truth. A history of the theatre unfolds—one with no claim whatsoever to objectivity—told by men and women who have answered the stage's siren song. Philosophers, novelists, historical figures, and just plain folk make cameo appearances when they, too, can contribute to the play.

Places, please.

THE
THEATRE
QUOTATION
BOOK

PROLOGUE:
Art's Nature and Purpose

We have art so that we must not die of the truth.
FRIEDRICH NIETZSCHE

Art is the lie that leads to truth.
PABLO PICASSO

Most people mistake the fetish for accuracy with truth.
EUGÈNE DELACROIX

That is not the truth. That is just a fact. The truth is what the facts mean.
SAM, in *Traveler in the Dark* by Marsha Norman

Tolstoy used to say he had found truth. Personally, I don't understand anything. You ask me, "What is life?" It's as though you asked me, "What is a carrot?" A carrot is a carrot and beyond that nobody knows. All I can do is show man what he is. . . and then let him figure out what he's watching.
ANTON CHEKHOV

I cannot bear Shakespeare, you know, but your plays are even worse. Shakespeare takes the reader by the neck and leads him to a certain goal, and does not let him turn aside. And where is one to go with your heroes? From the sofa where they are lying to the closet and back.

LEV TOSTOY, to Anton Chekhov

In my opinion, my opinions are the correct opinions to have, but having the correct opinions is not the same as knowing the truth, having Wisdom; some people have that, but I don't know where they got it any more than I know, really, why I'm gay.

TONY KUSHNER

Now, for the poet, he nothing affirms, and therefore never lieth. For, as I take it, to lie is to affirm that to be true which is false.

PHILIP SIDNEY

The truest poetry is the most feigning.

TOUCHSTONE, in *As You Like It* by William Shakespeare

2

Shakespeare is in the singularly fortunate position of being, to all intents and purposes, anonymous.
    W. H. AUDEN

Poetry is the spontaneous overflow of powerful feelings.
    WILLIAM WORDSWORTH

Ceremonies are the outward expression of inward feeling.
    LAO-TZU

Art is a means of escape from the pain of desire.
    ARTHUR SCHOPENHAUER

All Arts contribute to the greatest art of all: *Lebenskunst*—the art of getting through life.
    BERTOLT BRECHT

A work of art is not about life, it has life.
    W. H. AUDEN

The difference between Art and Life is that Art is more bearable.

CHARLES BUKOWSKI

Art gives meaning to matter and form to the formless.

ANONYMOUS

Form follows function.

LOUIS SULLIVAN

Art is not a cocktail party: it's a tankful of sharks. Nothing's just for exercise, everything's for keeps.

JOHN GARDNER

Art is something of its own and not something of something else. It is not education, it is not social betterment, it is not about civic pride or better international relations or group therapy.

ZELDA FICHANDLER

The artist is an imitator and, like all other imitators, is thrice removed from the truth.

PLATO

Not to know that a young deer has no horn is a less serious matter than to paint it inartistically.

ARISTOTLE

The artist knows nothing of the reality, only the appearance.

PLATO

The poet should prefer probable impossibilities to improbable possibilities.

ARISTOTLE

The poet's creations are poor things by the standards of truth and reality, and his appeal is not to the highest part of the soul.

PLATO

Poetry, therefore, is more philosophical and graver than history: for poetry tends to express the universal, history the particular.

ARISTOTLE

The artist will go on imitating only what pleases the taste or wins approval of the ignorant multitude.

PLATO

Plato is dear to me, but truth is dearer still.

ARISTOTLE

All art is but imitation of nature.

SENECA

It is better to invent reality than to copy it.

GIUSEPPE VERDI

A copy of the universe is not what is required of art; one of the damned thing is ample.

REBECCA WEST

Art is not the reflection of reality, it is the reality of that reflection.

JEAN-LUC GODDARD

What you call the spirit of the age is in reality one's own spirit in which the age is mirrored.

JOHANN WOLFGANG VON GOETHE

The artist's surroundings are unimportant. He lives inside his own head.

BENVENUTO CELLINI

If an artist only saw things as they were, he would cease to be an artist.

OSCAR WILDE

If the world were clear, art would not exist. Art helps us pierce the opacity of the world.

ALBERT CAMUS

Artworks clearly are superior to all other things; since they stay longer in the world than anything else, they are the worldliness of things.

HANNAH ARENDT

ACT ONE
Scene One:
The Theatre World...and America

Totus mundus agit histrionem.
(All the world's a stage.)
> GLOBE THEATRE MOTTO, displayed outside the theatre on a sign with Hercules holding up the earth

There is that smaller world which is the stage, and that larger stage which is the world.
> ISAAC GOLDBERG

There is no surer method of evading the world than by following art, and no surer method of linking oneself to it than by art.
> JOHANN WOLFGANG VON GOETHE

The theatre is an escape from reality.
> GEORGE JEAN NATHAN

The theatre is the first serum that man invented to protect himself from the sickness of despair.
> JEAN-LOUIS BARRAULT

The theatre is not so much a profession as a disease, and my first look at Broadway was the beginning of a lifelong infection.

MOSS HART

The basis of drama is any form or rhythm imposed upon the world of action.

T. S. ELIOT

Theatre is what literature does at night.

GEORGE JEAN NATHAN

Theatre: poor stepsister of the arts.

PHILIP SIDNEY

One goes to the theatre to find life, but if there is no difference between life outside the theatre and life inside, then theatre makes no sense. There's no point doing it.

PETER BROOK

It is the spectator, and not life, that art really mirrors.

OSCAR WILDE

[Theatre] exists not just to make a mirror of life, but to represent a kind of realm just as certainly as music is a realm.

JOSEPH CHAIKIN

Art is not a mirror to reflect society, but a hammer with which to shape it.

LEON TROTSKY

Theatre takes place all around us and it is the purpose of the formal theatre to remind us this is so.

JOHN CAGE

Drama is life with the dull bits cut out.

ALFRED HITCHCOCK

Myths are made for the imagination to breathe life into them.

ALBERT CAMUS

Imagination rules the world.

NAPOLEON

I am an enthusiast on the subject of the arts. But it is an enthusiasm of which I am not ashamed, as its object is to improve the taste of my countrymen, to increase their reputation, to reconcile to them the respect of the world, and produce for them its praise.

THOMAS JEFFERSON

The life of the arts, far from being an interruption, a distraction in the life of a nation, is very close to the center of a nation's purpose, and is a test of the quality of a nation's civilization.

JOHN F. KENNEDY

The only music Jack liked was "Hail to the Chief."

JACQUELINE KENNEDY

In aristocracies, a few great pictures are produced; in democratic countries, a vast number of insignificant ones.

ALEXIS DE TOCQUEVILLE

Celebrity is democracy's substitute for aristocracy.

JOHN LAHR

What is the function of art but to preserve in permanent and beautiful form those emotions and solaces which cheer life and make it kindlier, more heroic and easier to comprehend; which lift the mind of the worker from the harshness and loneliness of his tasks, and, by connecting him with what has gone before, free him from a sense of isolation and hardship.

JANE ADDAMS

Art must be the handmaiden of sublimity and beauty and thus promote whatever is natural and healthy.

ADOLPH HITLER

Beauty will not come at the call of the legislature.

RALPH WALDO EMERSON

Congressman Joseph Starnes: You are quoting from this Marlowe. Is he a communist?
Hallie Flanagan: I was quoting from Christopher Marlowe.
Starnes: Tell us who Marlowe is so we can get the proper references, because that is all we want to do.

13

Flanagan: Put in the record that he was the greatest dramatist in the period of Shakespeare, immediately preceding Shakespeare.

TESTIMONY BEFORE THE HOUSE COMMITTEE TO INVESTIGATE UN-AMERICAN ACTIVITIES, 1939

The theatre in New York is indirectly subsidized by the Bureau of Internal Revenue, which considers "entertainment" a tax deductible business expense for the thousands of business executives and buyers who stream into the city annually.

LEE SIMONSON, 1963

Art is a nation's most precious heritage. For it is in our works of art that we reveal to ourselves, and to others, the inner vision which guides us as a Nation. And where there is no vision, the people perish.

LYNDON JOHNSON, signing the bill creating the National Endowment for the Arts, 1965

Artists have to be brave; they live in the realm of ideas and expression of their ideas will often be provocative and unusual. Artists stretch the

14

limits of understanding. They express ideas that are sometimes unpopular. In an atmosphere of liberty, artists and patrons are free to think the unthinkable and create the audacious. They are free to make both horrendous mistakes and glorious celebrations.

RONALD REAGAN

Thus, for FY 1982, President Reagan's budget request of $88 million was a far cry from the previous year's appropriation of $158.8 million and even further from the projected authorization level of $190 million.

MARGARET JANE WYSZOMIRSKI

We ask that the Senate stop all funding to the National Endowment for the Arts, or provide equal funding for all other groups of artists—carpenters, brick masons, truck drivers, sales clerks, etc. It is inconceivable that a Senator would vote to give $171 million for projects such as those of Serrano or Mapplethorpe.

AMERICAN FAMILY ASSOCIATION press release
(Rev. Donald Wildmon, Executive Director), 1989

Artists are society's watchers, critics, and champions. They speak the unspeakable, even if it manifests itself in horrifying, untidy, or esoteric manners. . . . Art that challenges existing prejudices serves a most important function; it helps us grow and reach a higher state of humanity.

CONGRESSMAN TED WEISS, 1990

Projects, productions, workshops, and programs that are determined to be obscene are prohibited from receiving financial assistance under this Act from the National Endowment for the Arts.

AMENDMENT TO SECTION 5(d) OF THE NATIONAL FOUNDATION ON THE ARTS AND THE HUMANITIES ACT OF 1965 (20 U.S.C. 954[d]), passed by Congress, 1990

If you give artists freedom of expression, soon every American will want it.

ANONYMOUS, banner protesting legal action against the Contemporary Arts Center of Cincinnati, 1990

The homosexual "community," the feminists, the civil libertarians, the pro-abortionists, the flag burners and many other fringe political groups are more active than ever in promoting their dangerous anti-family and anti-American agendas. They are battling us on every front! . . . I believe that if you alert your friends and supporters regarding how the NEA is using American taxpayers' dollars, it will make a difference.

SENATOR JESSE HELMS, letter to Rev. Jerry Falwell, 1991

A statute disfavoring speech that fails to respect Americans' "diverse beliefs and values" is the very model of viewpoint discrimination.

SUPREME COURT JUSTICE DAVID H. SOUTER, in the sole dissenting opinion to the 1998 Supreme Court ruling that upheld the 1990 Congressional amendment to the National Foundation on the Arts and the Humanities Act

Censorship is to art what lynching is to justice.

HENRY LOUIS GATES

"Mary H. Magdalen."

MARTHA, speaking the line approved by the Lord Chamberlain to substitute for the original "Jesus H. Christ" in the London production of *Who's Afraid of Virginia Woolf?* by Edward Albee

No one fights over a dead art or a dead issue.
HALLIE FLANAGAN

That government which governs least, governs best.
THOMAS JEFFERSON

The broadest stream of American cultural influence did not stem from Jefferson, who in his middle years made himself a cultivated autodidact, but from Puritan New England. One did not pleasure oneself with pleasure. The aesthetic, the artifacts of creativity had to be good for you, good for something, good for education, for social uplift.
W. MCNEIL LOWRY

I'm going on the theory that the United States, instead of being the most successful country in the world, is the greatest failure because it was given everything more than any other country.
EUGENE O'NEILL

Democratic nations will habitually prefer the useful to the beautiful, and they will require that the beautiful be useful.
ALEXIS DE TOCQUEVILLE

ACT ONE
Scene Two:
Theatre's Purpose ...and Its Opponents

Art has as much reason for being as the earth
and the sun.

RALPH WALDO EMERSON

Nothing is more useful to men than those arts
that have no utility.

OVID

Art, unlike a tool, does not disappear into use-
fulness.

MARTIN HEIDEGGER

How can the theatre be both entertaining and
instructive at the same time?

BERTOLT BRECHT

The poet's aim is either to profit or to please,
or to blend in one the delightful and the useful.

HORACE

When Horace expresses the most common-place thought and the most trivial feeling, they sound magnificent. That's because he worked with marble. Nowadays, we work with shit.

BERTOLT BRECHT

The technical word used to bring out a play was "to teach," and the technical name for the director of the performance was *didascalus* or "teacher."

ROY FLICKINGER

And if our pen in this seeme over slight,
We strive not to instruct but to delight.

Prologue to *The Dutch Courtesan* by John Marston

The end of writing is to instruct; the end of poetry is to instruct by pleasing.

SAMUEL JOHNSON

The function of the theatre is not to teach, but to pose questions. The worst thing is when social and moral teachings come from the stage. When there is already an answer, it ceases to be theatre.

GEORGE TOUSTONOGOV

The business of plays is to recommend virtue and discountenance vice; to shew the uncertainty of human greatness, the sudden turns of fate, and the unhappy conclusions of violence and injustice.

JEREMY COLLIER

Good politics always make bad art.

PETER HALL

All disobedience to the creative life of the theatre is a crime.

KONSTANTIN STANISLAVKSY

A human being starts conquering a situation when he speaks word about it.

BERTOLT BRECHT

All we need for evil to win in the world is for good people to do nothing.

EDMUND BURKE

Among theatre folk the activist impulse is forever devoured, or rather eviscerated, by our fatal attraction to its inherent drama. We love the flash and thunderclap and are too impa-

tient to do the work of constructing the bomb.
TONY KUSHNER

When Auden said his poetry didn't save one Jew from the gas chamber, he'd said it all. I never felt this, that art is important. That's been my secret guilt, and I think it is the secret guilt of most artists.
TOM STOPPARD

I fear those who seek tendencies between the lines and who without fail wish to see me as a liberal or a conservative. I am not a liberal, not a conservative, not a gradualist, not a monk, and not an indifferentist. I would like to be a free artist—and that's all, and the only thing I regret is that God has not given me the forces to be one.
ANTON CHEKHOV

I am more the poet and less the social philosopher than people have generally been inclined to believe.
HENRIK IBSEN

I try to take settings and dramatic situations

from life which involve real questions of right and wrong. Then I set out, rather implacably and in the most realistic situations I can find, the moral dilemma and try to point a real, though hard, path out. I don't see how you can write anything decent without using the question of right and wrong.

ARTHUR MILLER

Why do people always expect authors to answer questions? I am an author because I want to ask questions. If I had answers I'd be a politician.

EUGÈNE IONESCO

Theatre is not, after all, the post office, primarily designed for the conveyance of messages.

FRANK KERMODE

The best theatre is a kind of courtroom with the society on trial.

KENNETH TYNAN

It annoys me to see people comfortable when they ought to be uncomfortable; and I insist on making them think in order to bring them to conviction of sin.

GEORGE BERNARD SHAW

I think the job of art by and large at the moment, especially the theatre, is not to reconcile people, but to disturb them, to hassle them, to shake them out of their complacencies.

EDWARD BOND

My main concern is theatre; and the theatre does not reflect or mirror society. It has been stingy and selfish and it has to do better.

ANNA DEAVERE SMITH

On the one hand, both art and the artist are made to appear as secondary to another goal— education, community uplift, urban renewal, business itself. On the other is art as both creative and sacral and the artist as a man or woman with a profession, a vocation, a craft with its own self-imposed standards.

W. MCNEIL LOWRY

I have faith in theatre as the place where a community hears words that they can accept or reject, words that might help them to make decisions about their personal lives and their social responsibilities.

GIORGIO STREHLER

To art's subjectmatter, we should be more or less indifferent.

OSCAR WILDE

The subject of every play ought to be that men change.

JEAN-PAUL SARTRE

I wasn't in the theatre to be entertained—I was in it to be changed.

ROSEMARIE TICHLER

There is no man who differs more from another than he does from himself at another time.

BLAISE PASCAL

Comedy, like other forms of literature, has endured because it pleases: but philosophers have ever been loath to accept a hedonistic justification, and comic poets, when driven to defend themselves, have usually chosen to claim a moral function, and to say that if they did not always, like tragic writers, punish vice, they at least discouraged it by making it ridiculous and by putting laughter on the side of virtue.

JOSEPH WOOD KRUTCH

The good ended happily, and the bad unhappily. That is what Fiction means.

MISS PRISM, in *The Importance of Being Earnest* by Oscar Wilde

Every artist is a moralist, though he need not preach.

GEORGE SANTAYANA

I find that people's eyes can be opened as well from the stage as from a pulpit. Especially as so many people no longer go to church.

HENRIK IBSEN

The nation's morals are like teeth: the more decayed they are the more it hurts to touch them.

GEORGE BERNARD SHAW

Dramatic poetry has a most formidable power
of corrupting even men of high character.

PLATO

One recurrent feature of the history of the theatre is the fact that outbursts of anti-theatrical
sentiment tend to coincide with the flourishing of the theatre itself.

JONAS BARISH

When any one of these pantomimic gentlemen, who are so clever that they can imitate
anything, comes to us, and proposes to perform, we will fall down and worship him as a
sweet and holy and wonderful being: but we
must also inform him that in our State such as
he are not permitted to exist. . . . And so when
we have anointed him with myrrh, and set a
garland of wool upon his head, we shall send
him away to another city.

PLATO

On stage are to be seen naught but fornication,
adultery, courtesan women, men pretending to
be women, and soft-limbed boys.

ST. JOHN CHRYSOSTOM, fourth century C.E.

Theatres—those Cages of Uncleanness and public schools of Debauchery!

ST. AUGUSTINE, fifth century C.E.

Amongst all the whole rabblement, common players in interludes are to be taken for rogues and punishment is appointed for them to bee burnte through the ear with an hot iron of an inch compass; and for the second fault, to be hanged as felon, &c. The reason is that their trade is such an idle, loitering life, a practice to all mischief.

JOHN NORTHBROOKE, 1577

It hath evermore been the notorious badge of prostituted Strumpets and the lewdest Harlots, to ramble abroad to Plays, to Playhouses; whither no honest, chaste or sober Girls or Women, but only branded Whores and infamous Adulteresses, did usually resort in ancient times.

WILLIAM PRYNNE, 1633

All great amusements are dangerous to the Christian life; but among all those that the world has invented, there is none more to be feared than the theatre.

BLAISE PASCAL, 1670

Once the apostle Paul had laid down universal love between all men as the foundation of his Christian community, the inevitable consequence in Christianity was the utmost intolerance towards all who remained outside of it.

SIGMUND FREUD

Whereas publike Sports doe not well agree with private Calamities, nor publike stage-players with the Season of Humiliation . . . while these sad Causes and set times of Humiliation doe continue, publike Stage-Plays shall cease and be forborne.

First Ordnance against Stage Plays and Interludes, 1642

All the women's part[s] to be acted . . . may be performed by women.

KING CHARLES II, reopening London Theatres, 1660

If there must be Strumpets, let Bridewell [Prison] be the Scene. Let them come not to

Prate, but to be Punish'd.
  JEREMY COLLIER, 1698

I'll come no more behind your scenes, David; for the silk stockings and white bosoms of your actresses excite my amorous propensities.
  SAMUEL JOHNSON, to David Garrick

When Hume's late for dinner, I know he's either having an affair or is lying dead in the street. I always hope it's the street.
  JESSICA TANDY, on husband Hume Cronyn

"Truth" in theatre is just as chameleon-like as in real life. Actually, there is no truth in theatre or in any other medium of performance; there is only its illusion.
  HUME CRONYN

The last holy brothel is the theatre; the last holy prostitute is the actor.
  ATHOL FUGARD

The most dramatic moment in the world is when the priest raises his hands in consecration.
  JEAN GENET

The English are not a very spiritual people, so they invented cricket to give them some idea of eternity.

GEORGE BERNARD SHAW

But everybody knows which comes first when it's a question of cricket or sex—all discerning people recognize that.

HAROLD PINTER

Forty-second Street is the end of the world, Hieronymus Bosch.

PETER HALL

Religion and art spring from the same root. Economics and art are strangers.

WILLA CATHER

To my mind the modern theatre is nothing but tradition and conventionality. . . . We need new forms, and if we can't have them we're better off with no theatre at all.

KONSTANTIN, in *The Seagull* by Anton Chekhov

In order to rejuvenate the art, we declared war on all the conventionalities of the theatre wherever they might occur—in the acting, in the properties, in the scenery, the costumes, the interpretation of the play, the curtain, or anywhere else in the play or the theatre. All that was new and that violated the usual customs of the theatre seemed beautiful and useful to us.

KONSTANTIN STANISLAVSKY

The drama dies unless it is rejuvenated by new life. We must put new blood into this corpse.

ÉMILE ZOLA

To save the theatre, the theatre must be destroyed, the actors and actresses must all die of the plague. They poison the air.

ELEANORA DUSE

I think the theatre must be reformed in its plays, its speaking, its acting and its scenery. That is to say, I think there is nothing good about it at present.

WILLIAM BUTLER YEATS

We must think about the theatre of the future. Everything that exists now in Spain is dead. Either the theatre must be changed fundamentally or it is finished forever. There is no other solution.

FEDERICO GARCÍA LORCA

I seek theatrical means for the ruin of the theatre as it exists today in France.

ANTONIN ARTAUD

I don't think the traditional form of theatre means anything any longer. Its significance is purely historic.

BERTOLT BRECHT

To find a form that accommodates the mess, that is the task of the artist now.

SAMUEL BECKETT

All through the world in order to save the theatre almost everything of the theatre still has to be swept away.

PETER BROOK

ACT ONE
Scene Three:
Writing Plays

I started writing for the theatre because I hated it.
> EUGÈNE IONESCO

I hate writing, but I love having written.
> DOROTHY PARKER

I hate writing. Fat white fingers excreting dirty black ink. Smudges. Shadows. Shit. Silence.
> BEN JONSON, in *Bingo: Scenes of Money and Death* by Edward Bond

No audience, no echo. That's part of one's death.
> VIRGINIA WOOLF

I swear fearfully at the conventions of the stage.
> ANTON CHEKHOV

The Russian dramatist is one who, walking through a cemetery, does not see the flowers on the graves. The American dramatist . . .

does not see the graves under the flowers.

GEORGE JEAN NATHAN

One begins with two people on a stage, and one of them had better say something pretty damn quick.

MOSS HART

Show me a congenital eavesdropper with the instincts of a Peeping Tom and I will show you the making of a dramatist.

KENNETH TYNAN

How did I become a writer? In the same way that a woman becomes a prostitute. First I did it to please myself, then I did it to please my friends, and finally I did it for money.

FERENC MOLNÁR

In 1653 minor dramatist Philippe Quinnault refused a pittance of only fifty crowns from the actors at the Hôtel [de Bourgogne] for his *Les Rivales* and "suggested that no down payment be made but that he should receive ten percent of the receipts of the first run of the play, after which the rights were to be vested in the company." The actors accepted his terms, and thereafter made royalty payments to playwrights.

EDWIN DUERR

A good many young writers make the mistake of enclosing a stamped, self-addressed envelope big enough for the manuscript to come back in. This is too much of a temptation.

RING LARDNER

I was the guy here when the paper was white.

MOSS HART

Don't write stage directions. If it is not apparent what the character is trying to accomplish by saying the line, telling us how the character said it or whether or not she moved to the couch isn't going to aid the case.

DAVID MAMET

Three irreplaceable stage directions: "Exit, pursued by a bear" (William Shakespeare, *The*

Winter's Tale); "The clock strikes as much as it likes" (Eugène Ionesco, *The Bald Soprano*); "Trying to look like Tolstoy" (Athol Fugard, *"Master Harold" . . . and the Boys*).

Robert Bresson: You know, movies need a beginning, middle, and end.
Jean-Luc Goddard: Yes, but not necessarily in that order.

The Plot, then, is the first principle, and, as it were, the soul of a tragedy. Character holds the second place. . . . Third in order is Thought. . . . Fourth among the elements enumerated comes Diction. . . . Of the remaining elements Song holds the chief place among the embellishments. The Spectacle has, indeed, an emotional attraction of its own, but, of all the parts, it is the least artistic and connected least with the art of poetry.

ARISTOTLE

It's hard enough for me to write what I want to write without me trying to write what you say

37

they want me to write which I don't want to write.

TENNESSEE WILLIAMS

Once I have my plot in mind, my janitor could write the play.

EUGÈNE SCRIBE

The structure of a play is always the story of how the birds came home to roost.

ARTHUR MILLER

Drama should not present new stories but new relationships.

FREDERICK HEBBEL

All drama until now has been in the form of a detective story.

EUGÈNE IONESCO

In Aristotelian drama the plot leads the hero into situations where he reveals his innermost being. All the incidents shown have the object of driving the hero into spiritual conflicts. It is a possibly blasphemous but quite useful comparison if one turns one's mind to the burlesque shows on Broadway, where the public, with yells of "Take it off!," forces the girls to expose their bodies more and more.

BERTOLT BRECHT

Get into the scene late, get out of the scene early. That's how *Glengarry* got started.

DAVID MAMET

A writer's task is to See.

HENRIK IBSEN

How can I know what I mean 'til I see what I say.

ANDRÉ GIDE

Writers write a book in order to find out why they write it.

ALAIN ROBBE-GRILLET

The only purpose of writing is better to enjoy life, or better to endure it.

SAMUEL JOHNSON

A writer goes to previous writers not for technique but for spirit.

D. H. LAWRENCE

He retained what he wanted, cut ruthlessly what he did not want, and wrote in new scenes as he saw fit. He had always acted like this. His admirers spoke of adaptation and re-writing; his opponents called this method plagiarism, piracy, shameless robbery.

LOTTE LENYA, on Bertolt Brecht creating *The Threepenny Opera* from John Gay's *The Beggar's Opera*

Immature artists imitate. Mature artists steal.

LIONEL TRILLING

If you copy from one author it's plagiarism, if you copy from two it's research.

WILLIAM MIZNER

We fail to know what are the first-rate qualities in Beaumont and Fletcher because we will only see in them second-rate Shakespeare.

ARTHUR MIZENER

40

The only thing that is not amateurish about the play I have written, is my refusal to read it to you.

FRANZ KAFKA, to Oscar Baum

I have seen *The Sunday Times*, *The Dispatch*, and *The Satirist*, all of which blow their little trumpets against unhappy me, most lustily. Either I must have grievously awakened the ire of all the "adapters" and their friends, or the drama must be decidedly bad. I haven't made up my mind yet, which of the two is the fact.

CHARLES DICKENS, following the opening of his first effort as a dramatist

The critics suppose that it is easy to write a play. They aren't aware that writing a good play is difficult and writing a bad one is twice as hard.

ANTON CHEKHOV

Writing a play is the most difficult thing a writer can do with a pen.

KENNETH TYNAN

Failure in the theatre is more dramatic and uglier than in any other form of writing. It costs so much, you feel so guilty.

LILLIAN HELLMAN

I am not a generic playwright. I am a woman playwright. And I would hope that my choice of words and my choice of characters and situations reflect my experience as a woman on the planet. I don't have anything that I can add to the masculine perception of the world. What I can add has to be from what I've experienced. And my perceptions and my syntax, my colloquialism, my preoccupations, are founded on race and gender.

NTOZAKE SHANGE

If only a man can speak for a man, a woman for a woman, a Black person for all Black people, then we, once again, inhibit the spirit of the theatre.

ANNA DEAVERE SMITH

If the nature of human experience changes

with the color of a man's skin, then the racists have been right all along.

ATHOL FUGARD

Racial intolerance finds stronger expression, strange to say, in regard to small differences than to fundamental ones.

SIGMUND FREUD

I was so delirious that I drank a glass of water, thought it wine and got gloriously drunk. Negroes were at last on Broadway, and there to stay. Gone was the uff-dah of the minstrel! Gone was the Massa Linkum stuff! We were artists and we were going a long, long way. We had the world on a string tied to a runnin' red-geared wagon on a downhill pull. Nothing could stop us, and nothing did for a decade.

WILL MARION COOK, after opening *Clorindy*, or *The Origin of the Cakewalk*, 1898

If a man writes a play and a good play, he is lucky if he earns first class postage upon it. Of course, he may sell it commercially to some producer on Broadway but in that case it would not be a Negro play. Or if it is a Negro play, it will not be about the kind of Negro you and I want to know.

W. E. B. DU BOIS

I am very worried about the state of the civilization that produced that photograph of the white cop standing on that Negro woman's neck in Birmingham.

LORRAINE HANSBERRY, speaking to Attorney General Robert F. Kennedy, as reported by James Baldwin

My sense of responsibility is not to the American theatre, it is to the figures who are in the play.

SUZAN-LORI PARKS

Women's writing. Men's writing. Gay and lesbian writing. Black writing. Such categories are only literary apartheid that marginalizes specific groups of writers. They are false commercial distinctions that have nothing to do with the quality of writing. There are only two kinds of writing. Good and bad.

AISHA RAHMAN

I am keenly aware of the dangers of the political category, of appearing to have a good liberal conscience in an ugly situation. This cheapest of all pigeonholes has by and large been mine.

ATHOL FUGARD

There is no writer who can accept relegation to a ghetto happily. Like any other writer, we want to be universally heard.

LARRY KRAMER

No, there is no such thing as a gay sensibility, and yes, it has an enormous impact on our culture.

JEFF WEINSTEIN

A gay play is a play that sleeps with other plays of the same sex.

ROBERT PATRICK

I did not set out opportunistically to write about AIDS because it's such *great material:* but it is, isn't it? . . . [*Angels in America*] has also made me comfortable. And there's something unbearable about that. Which, maybe, I ought to keep to myself, but, playwright, theatre worker that I am, I am too much in love with the drama of declaration and mortification.

TONY KUSHNER

Playwriting isn't a calling as much as it is a hazing process.

PAULA VOGEL

Play-writing, like begging in India, is an honorable but humbling profession.

MOSS HART

We never have enough good plays, and the reason for that is we don't have enough bad plays. If we had a *lot* more bad plays, then we might have a few more good plays. The history of the theatre is the history of bad plays.

HAROLD CLURMAN

You ask me if I've written a play. Who the hell hasn't?

ERNEST HEMINGWAY, to Harold Clurman

The writer is the person for whom writing is more difficult than it is for other people.

THOMAS MANN

When I stepped from hard manual work to writing, I just stepped from one kind of hard work to another.

SEAN O'CASEY

Most modern plays are concerned with the relation between man and man, but that does not interest me at all. I am interested only in the relation between man and God.

EUGENE O'NEILL

To live is to battle with the trolls within the mind and heart. To write is to sit in judgment on oneself.

HENRIK IBSEN

To write a drama is to follow a thought to its conclusion.

GEORG KAISER

Who knows if Shakespeare might have thought less if he had read more.

EDWARD YOUNG

Words are very rascals. . . . Words are grown so false I am loath to prove reason with them.

FESTE, in *Twelfth Night* by William Shakespeare

When ideas fail, words come in very handy.

JOHANN WOLFGANG VON GOETHE

Genuine poetry can communicate before it is understood.

T. S. ELIOT

Rhetoric proceeds from the quarrel with others, poetry from the quarrel with ourselves.

WILLIAM BUTLER YEATS

I write plays because dialogue is the most respectable way of contradicting myself.

TOM STOPPARD

As a writer one is allowed to have conversations with oneself. What is considered sane in writers is mad for the rest of the human race.

ALAN AYCKBOURN

When Frederick had finished, they all applauded.
"But Frederick," they said, "you are a poet!"
Frederick blushed, took a bow, and said shyly, "I know it."

LEO LIONNI

I think like a genius, I write like a distinguished author, and I speak like a child.

VLADIMIR NABOKOV

When audiences come to see us authors lecture, it is largely in the hope that we'll be funnier to look at than to read.

SINCLAIR LEWIS

It's better to keep your mouth shut and appear stupid than to open it and remove all doubt.

MARK TWAIN

It is quite true that my plays are all talk, just as Raphael's pictures are all paint, Michelangelo's statues are all marble, Beethoven's symphonies all noise.

GEORGE BERNARD SHAW

Every word is like an unnecessary stain on silence and nothingness.

SAMUEL BECKETT

The more acute the experience, the less articulate its expression.

HAROLD PINTER

Everything that can be said can be said clearly.

LUDWIG WITTGENSTEIN

Human language is a cracked kettle on which we beat out tunes for bears to dance to, when all the while we wish to move the stars to pity.

GUSTAV FLAUBERT

One child was not satisfied with the attention paid her enraptured performance by the others, they were too involved in their own performances to suit her, so she stretched out her skinny arms and threw back her skinny neck and shrieked to the deaf heavens and her equally oblivious playmates, "Look at me, look at me, look at me!" . . . I wonder if she is not, now, a Southern writer.

TENNESSEE WILLIAMS

Trust the book, don't trust the writer. The writer's a damn liar.

D. H. LAWRENCE

It isn't a shortage of good scripts that ails the theatre, it is a shortage of producers who know a good script when they see one.

GEORGE JEAN NATHAN

I once asked a producer whether he received many scripts. He replied, "Plenty of scripts, but very few plays."

CHARLES DULLIN

It would mean sitting under the reproachful eyes of all those scripts I ought to have read.

THE DRAMATURG, in *The Messingkauf Dialogues* by Bertolt Brecht

A literary manager is a theatre's court jester: the person who lobbies against the plays that are done and for the ones that aren't.

LES GOTTHOLD

ACT ONE
Scene Four:
Genres —Tragedy, Comedy, Musicals, and More

Aeschylus: What is the playwright's duty, and why is he admired?
Euripides: Because he can write, and because he can think, but mostly because he makes men better in the city-states.

In *The Frogs* by Aristophanes

Tragedy, then, is an imitation of an action that is serious, complete, and of a certain magnitude; in language embellished with each kind of artistic ornament, the several kinds being found in separate parts of the play; in the form of action, not of narrative; through pity and fear effecting the proper purgation of these emotions.

ARISTOTLE

Where Aristotle fails us as a theatre critic is in saying excessively little about acting and staging.

A. C. WARD

Drama has to do with circumstance, tragedy has to do with individual choice.

DAVID MAMET

Yet tragic experience, because of its central importance, commonly attracts the fundamental beliefs and tensions of a period, and tragic theory is interesting mainly in this sense, that through it the shape and set of a particular culture is often deeply realized.

RAYMOND WILLIAMS

It is certainly not the least charm of a theory that it is refutable.

FRIEDRICH NIETZSCHE

In tragedy the protagonists die, but the moral order is preserved.

JAN KOTT

The hero is isolated, but not only from men; he also abandons, or feels himself abandoned by, the gods.

BERNARD KNOX

Show me a hero and I'll write you a tragedy.

F. SCOTT FITZGERALD

Happy is the country that needs no heroes.

BERTOLT BRECHT

The tragic hero is a scapegoat. A scapegoat is a sign, a symbol, and a figure of mediation. The tragic opposition exists between suffering, which does not justify anything, and myth, which justifies all.

JAN KOTT

One can play comedy, two are required for melodrama, but a tragedy demands three.

ELBERT HUBBARD

All tragedies are finish'd by a death,
All comedies are ended by a marriage;

The future states of both are left to faith.

BYRON, GEORGE GORDON, LORD

The world is a comedy to those that think, a tragedy to those that feel.

HORACE WALPOLE

Deep thinking is attainable only by a man of deep feeling.

SAMUEL TAYLOR COLERIDGE

Life is not tragic. Life is ridiculous. And that cannot be borne.

HENRIK IBSEN

Jokes die with their subjects; that is the tragedy of comedy.

PETER ARNOTT

Voltaire said that heaven has given us two things to compensate us for the many miseries of life—home and sleep. He might have added laughter to the list.

IMMANUEL KANT

He deserves paradise who makes his companions laugh.

THE KORAN

Existence itself, the act of existing, is a striving, and is both pathetic and comic in the same degree.

SØREN KIERKEGAARD

Comedy has to hurry to lower the curtain in the moment of joy so that we don't see what comes afterwards.

ARTHUR SCHOPENHAUER

The comic and the tragic views of life no longer exclude each other.

WYLIE SYPHER

My tragedies are funnier than my comedies. Some of these characters have to laugh. They've got to. Or they'll die.

TENNESSEE WILLIAMS

The sight of other people in trouble is nearly always funny. . . . Nearly all of my successful songs have been based on the idea that I am getting the worst of it.

BERT WILLIAMS

Nothing is funnier than unhappiness, I grant you that.

NELL, in *Endgame* by Samuel Beckett

In moments of joy the Irish are comforted by the fact that tragedy lurks around the corner.

WILLIAM BUTLER YEATS

Some of you people aren't happy unless you're miserable.

MAIRE, in *Translations* by Brian Friel

Every love, happy as well as unhappy, is a real disaster.

IVAN TURGENEV

One must have a heart of stone to read the death of Little Nell of Dickens without laughing.

OSCAR WILDE

Men show their character in nothing more clearly than by what they think laughable.

JOHANN WOLFGANG VON GOETHE

Number one rule: I don't draw a distinction between comedy and drama. If it ain't funny, it ain't real, and if it ain't real, it ain't going to be funny.

LINDA LAVIN

My way of joking is to tell the truth. It is the funniest thing in the world.

GEORGE BERNARD SHAW

Perhaps you think I am joking. I am never so serious as when I am.

ROBERT FROST

You would hardly appreciate the comic if you felt yourself isolated from others. Laughter appears to stand in need of an echo.

HENRI BERGSON

You grow up the day you have the first real laugh—at yourself.

ETHYL BARRYMORE

It's an odd calling to make decent folk laugh.

MOLIÈRE

The source of Molière's wit is clear reason; it is a fountain of that soil, and it springs to vindicate reason, common sense, rightness, and justice—for no vain purpose ever.

GEORGE MEREDITH

It infuriates me to be wrong when I know I'm right.

MOLIÈRE

Every comic character is a type. Inversely, every resemblance to a type has something comic to it.

HENRÍ BERGSON

A learned fool is more foolish than an ignorant fool.

MOLIÈRE

Comedy for Molière was an end and not a means.

W.G. MOORE

Comedy too is acquainted with justice.

ARISTOPHANES

What Martin Luther King is doing with love, I am trying to do with laughter.

OSSIE DAVIS

Nor is the moving of laughter always the end of comedy, that is rather a fowling for the people's delight, or their fooling.

BEN JONSON

The tendency of comedy is to include as many people as possible in its final society: the blocking characters are more often reconciled or converted than simply repudiated.

NORTHROP FRYE

My point of view is primarily comic in that I see a reconciliation possible at the play's end between the individual and the world. And that's not terribly American. If you look at the European tradition—Molière, Coward, Congreve—the world is always put back together by the end. In American comedies, there's anarchism at the end.

A. R. GURNEY

In truth, no age has so fallen victim to the comic as this.

SØREN KIERKEGAARD

One excellent test of the civilization of a country I take to be the flourishing of the comic idea and comedy; and the test of true comedy is that it shall awaken thoughtful laughter.

GEORGE MEREDITH

The profession of a jester, like that of an intellectual, consists in providing entertainment.

JAN KOTT

Copernicus is a comic because he took apart, not the machine of the universe, but what we think of it.

LUIGI PIRANDELLO

Pirandello's plays are grenades that explode in

the mind of the spectator, causing all preconceived ideas of reality to collapse.

ANTONIO GRAMSCI

Criticism makes art sound more intellectual than it is.

JOHN GARDNER

In view of the human condition, the only sustainable posture is one of humor.

LUIGI PIRANDELLO

The essence of Pirandello is not his intellectuality. It is his conversion of the intellect into passion.

ERIC BENTLEY

An intellectual is someone who turns answers into questions.

HAROLD ROSENBERG

Somehow it seems to fill my head with ideas—only I don't exactly know what they are.

ALICE, in *Through the Looking Glass* by Lewis Carroll

Genuine humor and true wit require a sound and capacious mind, which is always a grave one.

WALTER SAVAGE LANDOR

The philosopher and comic poet are of a cousinship in the eye they cast on life; and they are equally unpopular with our willful English of the hazy region and the ideal that is not to be disturbed.

GEORGE MEREDITH

In the United States the play of the mind is perhaps the only form of play that is not looked upon with the most tender indulgence.

RICHARD HOFSTADTER

Our theatre exists in carefully fostered isolation from the intellectual life of the country.

FRANCIS FERGUSSON

American society is generally suspicious of ideas.

LIONEL TRILLING

It would be a very good thing if the theatre took itself seriously as a factory of thought, a prompter of conscience, an elucidator of social conduct, an armory against despair and dullness, and a temple of the Ascent of Man.

GEORGE BERNARD SHAW

The tree of life is greener than the tree of thought.

FRIEDRICH HEGEL

We think about the play, but we enjoy the show.

HAROLD CLURMAN

The best actors in the world, either for tragedy, comedy, history, pastoral, pastoral-comical, historical-pastoral, tragical-historical, tragical-comical-historical-pastoral, scene individable or poem unlimited.

POLONIUS, on the visiting troupe in *Hamlet* by William Shakespeare

If a play does anything—either tragically or comically, satirically or farcically—to explain to me why I am alive, it is a good play. If it seems unaware that such questions exist, I tend to suspect that it is a bad one.

KENNETH TYNAN

Satire is what closes Saturday night.

GEORGE S. KAUFMAN

The end of satire is the first alarm bell signaling the end of real democracy.

VLADIMIR MAYAKOVSKY

We are circus ringmasters and we can be found whistling amongst the winds of fairgrounds, in convents, prostitutions, theatres, realities, feelings, restaurants, ohoho, bang bang.

TRISTAN TZARA

Shit!

PA UBU, in the play by Alfred Jarry, first recorded use of the word on stage

In farce, as in drama, one is permitted the outrage but spared the consequence.

ERIC BENTLEY

Farce is the essential theatre. Farce refined becomes high comedy; farce brutalized becomes tragedy.

GORDON CRAIG

When two of my characters should under no circumstances encounter one another, I throw them together as quickly as possible.

GEORGES FEYDEAU

To see a farcical comedy more than once is like drinking stale champagne.

JOSEPH HOLLOWAY

Farce is tragedy played at a thousand revolutions per minute.

JOHN MORTIMER

As love and hate, tragedy and farce are closely related. Tragedy is the farce that involves our sympathies, farce, the tragedy that happens to outsiders.

ALDOUS HUXLEY

I feel frustrated at the end of a farce, but elevated and high at the end of a tragedy.

ALBERT FINNEY

What is called realism is usually a record of life at a low pitch and ebb viewed in the sunless light of day.

WALTER DE LA MARE

Our stage will be naturalistic, or it will cease to exist.

ÉMILE ZOLA

Allusion has been made to [Proust's] contempt for the literature that "describes," for the realists and naturalists worshipping the offal of experience, prostrate before the epidermis and the swift epilepsy, and content to transcribe the surface, the façade, behind which the Idea is prisoner.

SAMUEL BECKETT

When you see a guy masturbating on stage, you think "Aha! That's naturalism."

DRAGAN KLAIC

The forces confronting each other in tragedy are equally legitimate, equally justified. In melodramas or dramas, on the other hand, only one force is legitimate.

ALBERT CAMUS

I have suggested that the characteristic melodramatic situations and plots derive directly from more or less paranoid fantasies—generally the fantasy of innocence surrounded by malevolence.

ERIC BENTLEY

When prose cannot say a thing, you turn to poetry. . . . When poetry can't say it, you must sing it out.

GIAN CARLO MENOTTI

Q: Are there differences between musical theatre and opera?
Jonathan Tunick: The attitude on casting in opera is you look for someone who can sing. In a musical you look for someone who can best play the role, and if the music needs adjusting that will be done. The cast of an

opera is chosen for the voice. The cast of a musical is chosen for acting and voice. (You will never see a middle-age ingenue in a musical.) It's the only dependable definition.

Remember that this country was founded by Puritans who were fleeing England, where the first thing they did in power was to close down the theatres. Plays could be performed if there was musical accompaniment, if they were called operas. In short, music was sacred, the theatre profane.

ROBERT BRUSTEIN

That which is alwaies accompanied with effeminate lust-provoking Musicke, is doubtless inexpedient and unlawfull unto Christians. But Stage-Players are always accompanied with such Musicke.

WILLIAM PRYNNE

Music unlocks the frozen rivers of the heart.

ANTON CHEKHOV

Musick has Charms to soothe a savage Breast.

ALMERIA, in *The Mourning Bride* by William Congreve

Molière is like humming an air one has heard performed by an accomplished violinist of the pure tones without flourish.

GEORGE MEREDITH

It is better to make a piece of music than to perform one, better to perform one than to listen to one, better to listen to one than to misuse it as a means of distraction, entertainment, or acquisition of "culture."

JOHN CAGE

In years past, Hollywood made movies from Broadway musicals, but Broadway itself was too creative to base its musicals on anything that originated in Hollywood. Today, except for Stephen Sondheim and Harold Prince, Broadway musicals are mostly rehashes of Hollywood movies.

JONATHAN REYNOLDS

If two wrongs didn't make a right, there would be no dinner theatre.

<small>BERNIE LINCICOME</small>

The question of how simple-minded the book of a musical comedy can be was debated last night, and the verdict arrived at was "no end."

<small>RICHARD WATTS, JR., on *The Desert Song*</small>

"Musical Comedy," the most glorious words in the English language.

<small>JULIAN MARSH, in *42nd Street* by Bradford Ropes</small>

A musical comedy is a series of songs with jokes in between.

<small>STEPHEN SONDHEIM</small>

You want my opinion as though I didn't really know you? Well, it's the worst thing I've ever read.

<small>OSCAR HAMMERSTEIN II, responding to the first musical of his fifteen-year-old neighbor, Stephen Sondheim</small>

The idea of equipping a song-and-dance production with a few living, three-dimensional figures talking and behaving like human beings may no longer strike the boys in the business as merely fantastic.

WOLCOTT GIBBS, on *Pal Joey*

If you start with the right opening, you can ride for forty-five minutes on the telephone book. On the other hand, if you start off with a wrong one it's an uphill fight all the way.

OSCAR HAMMERSTEIN II, advising Stephen Sondheim

The four most dramatic words in the English language: "Act One, Scene One."

MOSS HART

America is the country of first acts.

VAN WYCK BROOKS

It is almost axiomatic that musicals have second-act troubles.

DENNY MARTIN FLINN

A musical is an organism bent on self-destruction.

TREVOR NUNN, to Richard Nelson

If Hitler is alive, I hope he's out of town with a musical.

LARRY GELBART

Zero Mostel, blacklisted during the McCarthy era, was gingerly canvassed about [bringing in a play doctor] as his animosity toward [Jerome] Robbins, who had named names in order to protect his career, was well known. "We of the left," Mostel informed the producers when they asked his permission, "have no blacklist."

DENNY MARTIN FLINN, on *A Funny Thing Happened on the Way to the Forum* out of town

Whoever cares most, wins.

JAMES LAPINE, describing "the Stephen Sondheim principle" of collaborating on a new show

Mostly we agreed, but when we didn't, the

"No" guy won.

Cy Feuer, on producing musicals with his partner,
Ernest Martin

Billy Rose: Your music great success STOP
Could be sensational success if you would
authorize Robert Russell Bennett retouch
orchestration STOP Bennett orchestrates even
the works of Cole Porter STOP
Igor Stravinsky: Satisfied with great success
STOP

Telegram exchange after Philadelphia opening of
Seven Lively Arts

Jerry Bock and I were asked the inevitable
question: "What comes first, the words or the
music?" Jerry's answer was, "The book."

Sheldon Harnick

As stage manager, the only things I didn't have
to worry about were singing the hit song or
selling orange drink in the lobby.

Ruth Mitchell

The knowledgeable lyricist avoids hard consonants at the end of phrases and especially at the end of a song when it is usually desirable for the singer to sustain the final note. I refer especially to final *d, t, b, f* sounds.

    Lehman Engel

Forcing actors to say their final syllables.

    George Abbott, describing "the magical Abbott touch"

Nothing is more revolting than when the actor pretends not to notice that he has left the level of plain speech and started to sing. The three levels—plain speech, heightened speech, and singing—must always remain distinct.

    Bertolt Brecht

Fuck the music. Sing the words.

    Jule Styne

You might be humming the melody, but nine times out of ten, the words came first and inspired that melody. You need to connect the mind to the heart. Lyrics do that.

MICHAEL JOHN LACHIUSA

Party Guest: I just love Jerome Kern's "Ol' Man River."

Mrs. Oscar Hammerstein: Jerome Kern did not write "Ol' Man River." My husband wrote "Ol' Man River." Jerome Kern wrote, "Dum-di-dah-dah, di-dum-di-dah-dah."

Characters write their own music.

JEROME KERN

There may be trouble ahead,
But while there's music, and moonlight, and
    love, and romance,
Let's face the music and dance.

IRVING BERLIN

Glamour in the theatre is usually twenty cho-rus girls in a line all doing the same thing. It is assumed that twenty women are more glam-orous than one.

PETER USTINOV

Get under a good man and work up.

ANONYMOUS, advice to chorus girls overheard by Kathryn Harkin

It has long been a subject of some remark that the arts attract the curious, the crotchety and the quirky. But dancing seems to be practiced largely by the downright perverted and deranged.

AGNES DE MILLE

You have to love dancing to stick to it. It gives you nothing back, no manuscripts to store away, no paintings to show on walls and maybe hang in museums, no poems to be printed and read, nothing but that single fleeting moment when you feel alive.

MERCE CUNNINGHAM

A choreographer is never afraid to move you around, while most directors have their mind on keeping you where you will be heard.

GWEN VERDON

You have fun. They have fun. It's kind of dirty.

GARLAND WRIGHT, on directing musicals

The finest musical theatre is, after all, a direct descendant of tacky operettas and vaudeville, with all its cheap jokes and bawdy lyrics.

ALBERT INNAURATO

A good actress lasts, but sex appeal does not.

BRIGITTE BARDOT

ACT ONE
Scene Five:
Training

Our bodies can be our best friends or worst enemies.

MICHAEL CHEKHOV

Art cannot be taught. To possess an art means to possess talent. That is something one has or has not. You can develop it by hard work, but to create a talent is impossible.

RICHARD BOLESLAVSKY

Talent is a prerequisite for the future professional.

WALLACE STEGNER

The important talent is the talent to develop one's talent.

HOWARD STEIN

As much has to be caught as is taught.

ERIC BENTLEY

By the work one knows the workman.

JEAN DE LA FONTAINE

They never ask how long the work took. They do ask who did it.

ARTHUR C. VANDENBROUCKE, SR.

A skilled craftsman leaves no traces.

LAO TZU

The distinction between the craftsman and the true artist is precisely between knowing what one can do and not knowing—which is why one occupation is safe and the other always incipiently dangerous.

JOHN FOWLES

Everything in the labor of art amounts to one thing: the difficult should become customary, the customary easy, and the easy beautiful.

KONSTANTIN STANISLAVSKY

Bad acting, like bad writing, has a remarkable uniformity, whether seen on the French,

German, Italian, or English stages; it all seems modeled after two or three types and those the least like types of good acting. The fault generally lies less in the bad imitation of a good model, than in the successful imitation of a bad model.

GEORGE LEWES

I am in the theatrical profession myself, my wife is in the theatrical profession, my children are in the theatrical profession. I had a dog that lived and died in it from a puppy. . . . There's genteel comedy in your walk and manner, juvenile tragedy in your eye, and touch-and-go farce in your laugh. . . . You'll do as well as if you had thought of nothing else but the lamps from your birth downwards.

MR. VINCENT CRUMMLES urging Nicholas Nickleby to become an actor, in the novel by Charles Dickens

Imagination! Imagination! I put it first years ago, when I was asked what qualities I thought necessary for success upon the stage. And I am still of the same opinion. Imagination, industry, and intelligence—"the three i's"—are all indispensable to the actress, but of these three the greatest is, without any doubt, imagination.

ELLEN TERRY

Imagination is more important than knowledge.

ALBERT EINSTEIN

It's in every human being to act. We're all "on" in a variety of ways, and some become very accomplished at it.

IAN MCKELLEN

Every sigh of Sarah Bernhardt, her tears, her convulsions in the death scenes, her entire acting is nothing but a cleverly learnt lesson.

ANTON CHEKHOV

Inspector of the actresses.

Chekhov's nickname within the Moscow Art Theatre, according to David Magarshack

I got all the schooling any actress needs. That is, I learned to write enough to sign contracts.
HERMIONE GINGOLD

I learned acting by doing it. And although I had never taken an acting class, it didn't take long to learn how to be on the stage. All you have to do is be humiliated in front of an audience a few times. If you don't like being humiliated publicly, you learn how to act.
RON VAWTER

When actors go onstage, you know immediately if they can do their job. You can be a lawyer or an accountat for years and not find out.
PATSY RODENBURG

Although the American upper classes have patronized artists, they have not encouraged their children to take up the arts as a serious career.
E. DIGBY BALTZELL

I must study politics and war that my sons may have liberty to study mathematics and philosophy. My sons ought to study mathematics and philosophy, geography, natural history and naval architecture, navigation, commerce and agriculture, in order to give their children a right to study painting, poetry, music, architecture, statuary, tapestry and porcelain.

JOHN ADAMS

[Shakespeare's sister] was as adventurous, as imaginative, as agog to see the world as he was. But she was not sent to school. She had no chance of learning grammar and logic, let alone of reading Horace and Virgil. She picked up a book now and then, one of her brother's perhaps, and read a few pages. But then her parents came in and told her to mend the stocking or mind the stew and not moon about with books and papers.

VIRGINIA WOOLF

Today, no American family can be secure against the danger that one of its children may decide to become an artist.

GARRISON KEILLOR

We should abolish all undergraduate art majors.

TONY KUSHNER

We have actors, but no art of acting.

GOTTHOLD LESSING

The main difference between the art of the actor and all other arts is that every other [non-performing] artist may create whenever he is in the mood of inspiration. But the artist of the stage must be the master of his own inspiration and must know how to call it forth at the hour announced on the posters of the theatre. This is the chief secret of our art.

KONSTANTIN STANISLAVSKY

The dualism that marks most artists sunders the actor, who is both the artist and the work of art.

TOBY COLE

Stanislavsky makes it very clear that while the actor's personal experience may be used as a

springboard for arousing the emotions required in the part, the emotions sought should
be those demanded by the role, in other words,
those of the character, and therefore not necessarily those which the actor would experience
at that moment.

CHRISTINE EDWARDS

The method of living a part in life demands
continual impromptu, while the technical
problem of learning a part by heart makes
impromptu acting impossible.

KONSTANTIN STANISLAVSKY

In the studio you learn to conform—to submit
yourself to the demands of your craft—so that
you may finally be free.

MARTHA GRAHAM

Even if empathy or self-identification with the
character can be usefully indulged in at
rehearsals . . . it has to be treated just as one of
a number of methods of observation.

BERTOLT BRECHT

87

The [Actors] Studio was organized in 1947 by Cheryl Crawford, Robert Lewis and Elias Kazan as a training ground for professional young actors. The hope and aim were to provide a place where the talented young actor could continue to work on problems of craft, correct errors and defects of approach or ability, and receive fresh stimuli toward new creativity.

LEE STRASBERG

The foundation for this method were my studies of the nature of an actor. The first [proposition] is this: there are no formulas.

KONSTANTIN STANISLAVSKY

I have therefore stressed the use of the word "Method" as against "System" to suggest that while we obviously are influenced by Stanislavsky's ideas and practices, we use it within the limitation of our own knowledge and experience.

LEE STRASBERG

I don't want any of that Stanislavsky shit from you!

CHARLES LAUGHTON, to Eli Wallach as they began rehearsals of *Major Barbara*

We were like converts to a new religion. We didn't understand anyone else's acting except our own. Everyone else was a pagan.

ELI WALLACH, on Lee Strasberg and the Actors Studio

Like the Bible, Stanislavsky's basic texts on acting can be quoted to any purpose.

LEE STRASBERG

I do think this ["Method"] train-ing would be wonderful for film actors, as the camera zeros in and captures two people being real together. But the problem in the theatre is being real fifty yards away. And that involves technique and skill—unfashionable terms these days.

LAURENCE OLIVIER

Playing Shakespeare requires technique. You don't play a Bach toccata by getting in the mood.

KEVIN KLINE

Playing Shakespeare is very tiring. You never get to sit down, unless you're a king.

JOSEPHINE HULL

The simplest examples of Stanislavsky's ideas are actors such as Gary Cooper, John Wayne and Spencer Tracy. They try not to act but to be themselves, to respond or react. They refuse to say or do anything they feel not to be consonant with their own character.

LEE STRASBERG

Steppenwolf is a collective. Our premise is to feel what people really feel. It doesn't require Stanislavsky or the Lee Strasberg stuff, the replacing a memory of how you felt when your dog got run over when you were eight. That's an insult to one's intelligence.

JOHN MALKOVICH

Nobody "becomes" a character. You can't act unless you are who you are.

MARLON BRANDO

Being another character is more interesting than being yourself.

JOHN GIELGUD

An actor has to be a clown to put himself in another's shoes.

GORDON CRAIG

There are no small parts, there are only small actors.

KONSTANTIN STANISLAVSKY

Are these 100 percent "living the part" folks really living the part, or are they living themselves and adding the author's words to that life? When they speak of "psychological truth" do they mean their psychology, or the truth of art which includes, in addition to true feeling, all the circumstances of the character, the situation, the style of the play, etc?

ROBERT LEWIS

What they call "the Method" is not generally advantageous to the actor at all. Instead of doing a scene over again that's giving them trouble, they want to discuss, discuss, discuss. I'd rather run through a scene eight times than waste time chattering away about abstractions. An actor gets a thing right by doing it over and over. Arguing about motivations and so forth is a lot of rot. American directors encourage that sort of thing too much.

LAURENCE OLIVIER

Lee Strasberg: What were you trying to do in the scene?
Mildred Dunnock: I was trying to do a damn fine performance.

Final words before stalking out of the Actors Studio, as told by Robert Lewis

Stanislavsky practiced psychology; Strasberg practices psychiatry. Staniskavsky's emotion came from the heart. Strasberg's comes from the kishkas.

VERA SOLOVIOVA

Lee makes me think. Lee says I have to begin to face my problems in my work and life.

    MARILYN MONROE

The more naïve and self-doubting the actors, the more total was Lee's power over them. The more famous and more successful these actors, the headier the taste of power for Lee. He found his perfect victim-devotee in Marilyn Monroe.

    ELIA KAZAN

Love the art in yourself rather than yourself in the art.

    KONSTANTIN STANISLAVSKY, from his autobiography, *My Life in Art*

Katharine Hepburn: You and Gadget [Elia Kazan] were the only ones mean and tough enough to come out of those ten years with the Group completely untouched.
Robert Lewis: Yes, except for two or three complete nervous breakdowns.

    —From *My Death in Art*, the working title of Lewis's autobiography, published as *Slings and Arrows*

Class, Lee Strasberg has died. Lee was a man of the theatre and I would like you to stand in his memory. (Pause.) You may sit. (Pause.) It will take the American theatre one hundred years to recover.

STELLA ADLER

The miniaturization or Americanization of the Stanislavsky method has become like the air we breathe, and like the air we breathe, we are rarely aware of its omnipresence.

ANNE BOGART

It is widely acknowledged to be the toughest job to get any two acting teachers to agree about anything.

ROBERT LEWIS

Most teachers of acting are frauds, and their schools offer nothing other than the right to consider oneself a part of the theatre.

DAVID MAMET

The most important thing you teach actors is to understand plays.

STELLA ADLER

[Adler's] celebrated script analysis course displayed a familiarity with dramatic literature well beyond the domestic play syllabus of most scene-study classes; her understanding of text exceeded that of most scholars.

ROBERT BRUSTEIN

A training process that focuses only on craft and skill development is a process that consciously desensitizes and neglects the intellectual, ethical and spiritual values of the artist. It creates product—actors as objects—not artistry.

JOHN HIRSCH

In most schools drama is taught as a suspiciously amusing branch of literature: we would gain much if it were taught as an offshoot of sociology.

KENNETH TYNAN

In much wisdom is much grief: and he that increaseth knowledge increaseth sorrow.

ECCLESIASTES

I wish I didn't know now what I didn't know then.

BOB SEEGER

Because of the poor condition of my memory, my education has never been a burden.

FLANNERY O'CONNOR

Ah me! What a burden knowledge is, where knowledge cannot avail.

TEIRESIAS, in *Oedipus Rex* by Sophocles

We know what we are, but know not what we may be.

OPHELIA, in *Hamlet* by William Shakespeare

ACT ONE
Scene Six:
Acting

The purpose of playing, whose end, both at the
first and now, was and is to hold, as 'twere, the
mirror up to nature.

    HAMLET, in the play by William Shakespeare

In the art of imitation there is the level of no
imitation. When the act of imitation is per-
fectly accomplished and the actor becomes the
thing itself, the actor will no longer have the
desire to imitate.

    ZEAMI MOTOKIYO

The actor should make you forget the existence of author and director, and even forget
the actor.

    PAUL SCOFIELD

These lines upon lines of print that call themselves plays are but inadequate records of the

full effect that author and actor conspired to produce.

HARLEY GRANVILLE-BARKER

At the moment of performance the text is supplied by the playwright, and the subtext by the actor.... If this were not the case, people would not go to the theatre but sit at home and read the play.

KONSTANTIN STANISLAVSKY

Actors in the theatre ... add so much to the ... poets that the verse moves us far more when heard than when read.... They succeed in securing a hearing even for the most worthless authors, who repeatedly win a welcome on the stage ... denied them in the library.

MARCUS FABIUS QUINTILIAN

I wanted, of course, to be an actor. It never occurred to me that these godlike creatures did not themselves make up the words that flowed so effortlessly and magnificently from their lips.

MOSS HART

A word is dead
When it is said,
Some say.
I say it just
Begins to live that day.
    EMILY DICKINSON

Actors should be judged by their voices.
    DEMOSTHENES

If we are to restore words to their sovereignty
we must have speech even more important
than gesture upon the stage
    WILLIAM BUTLER YEATS

Think Yiddish, speak British.
    STELLA ADLER

Every actor has a bad "s." Some are worse than
others.
    EDITH SKINNER

Good actors are good because of the things
they can tell us without talking. When they are

talking they are the slaves of the dramatist. It is what they can show the audience when they are not talking that reveals the fine actor.

CEDRIC HARDWICKE

The most precious things in speech are pauses.

RALPH RICHARDSON

People believe that mime is the art of silence, but this is seldom true. Usually it is endlessly talkative, because the performer daren't let his hold over the audience drop for one moment.

ETIENNE DECROUX

Ballet is the one form of theatre where nobody speaks a foolish word all evening—nobody on the stage at least. That's why it becomes so popular in any civilized country during a war.

EDWIN DENBY

Acting is imitation; when it ceases to be imitation it ceases to be acting and becomes something else—oratory perhaps, perhaps ballet dancing or posturing.

WILLIAM ARCHER

Acting is standing up naked and turning around very slowly.

ROSALIND RUSSELL

Acting is an outlet for neurotic impulses.

MARLON BRANDO

Acting is a masochistic form of exhibitionism. It is not quite the occupation of an adult.

LAURENCE OLIVIER

Acting will attract those who have excessive inner needs for, and urgent insatiable gratifications from, exhibiting themselves.

PHILIP WEISSMAN

Acting is half shame, half glory. Shame at exhibiting yourself, glory when you can forget yourself.

JOHN GIELGUD

Acting is the most minor of gifts. After all, Shirley Temple could do it when she was four.

KATHARINE HEPBURN

You never learn to act. By the time you learn to act you're too old to do it.

RUTH GORDON

When you are a personality, you don't need a personality.

MARSHA NORMAN

It takes a great deal of experience to become a natural.

WILLA CATHER

Julian Beck said that an actor has to be like Columbus: he has to go out and discover something, and come back and report on what he discovers.

JOSEPH CHAIKIN

A good actor makes clear the meaning of the words, a better actor gives also the emotion of the part, the best actor adds emotion of which the character is unconscious.

CLARE EAMES

Someone said of acting: Emotion is fun to indulge in, but it's boring to watch.

WILLIAM H. MACY

I find that I act best when my heart is warm and my head is cool.

JOSEPH JEFFERSON

Talent depends not, as you think, upon feeling, but upon rendering so exactly the outward signs of feeling.

DENIS DIDEROT

The actor does not let himself be transformed into the man he presents so that nothing of himself is left. He is not Lear, Harpagon, or the good solider Schweik—he is "showing" them to his audience.

BERTOLT BRECHT

The actor's job is to set himself on fire amidst the stage and wave at the audience through the flames.

ANTONIN ARTAUD

The whole motivation for any performer: "Look at me, Ma."

LENNY BRUCE

A ham is simply any actor who has not been successful in repressing his natural instincts.

GEORGE JEAN NATHAN

A coarse actor is one who can remember the lines but not the order in which they come.

MICHAEL GREEN

Very good actors never seem to talk about their art. Very bad ones never stop.

JOHN WHITING

The secret of acting is sincerity. Once you learn to fake that, you've got it made.

JEAN GIRAUDOUX, GROUCHO MARX, and/or GEORGE BURNS

In the theatre, lying is looked upon as an occupational disease.

TALLULAH BANKHEAD

Watching Tallulah Bankhead on stage is like watching somebody skating over very thin ice—and the English want to be there when she falls through.

    Mrs. Patrick Campbell

The fool cannot be a good actor, but a good actor can act the fool.

    Sophocles

Actors are the only honest hypocrites. . . . They wear the livery of other men's fortunes: their very thoughts are not their own.

    William Hazlitt

I really love actors, be-
cause they are the instrument for me, as precious
as a Stradivarius. An actor
is total carnality—all he
can use to get at you is
his body, his flesh, his
voice, his sense of self.

    Athol Fugard

It is the writer's job to make the play interesting. It is the actor's job to make the performance truthful.

DAVID MAMET

What is the talent of the actor? It is the art of counterfeiting himself, of putting on another character than his own, of appearing different than he is, of becoming passionate in cold blood, of saying what he does not think as naturally as if he really did think it, and finally, of forgetting his own place by dint of taking another's.

JEAN-JACQUES ROUSSEAU

Man is least himself when he talks in his own person. Give him a mask and he will tell you the truth.

OSCAR WILDE

The mask which an actor wears is apt to become his face.

PLATO

On the stage he was natural, simple, affecting;

'Twas only that when he was off he was acting.

OLIVER GOLDSMITH, on David Garrick

Nor Pen nor Pencil can the Actor save,
The Art and Artist, share one common Grave.

PROLOGUE to *The Clandestine Marriage* by George
Colman and David Garrick

Decay is inherent in all component things.

BUDDHA

An actor is a sculptor who carves in snow.

EDWIN BOOTH

Five stages in the life of an actor: 1) Who's
Mary Astor? 2) Get me Mary Astor. 3) Get
me a Mary Astor type. 4) Get me a young
Mary Astor. 5) Who's Mary Astor?

MARY ASTOR

For an actress to be a success she must have the
face of Venus, the brains of Minerva, the grace
of Terpsichore, the memory of Macaulay, the
figure of Juno, and the hide of a rhinoceros.

ETHEL BARRYMORE

The great discrimination of a dramatic critic is shown if he knows how to distinguish infallibly, in every case of satisfaction or dissatisfaction, what and how much of this is to be placed to the account of the poet or the actor. To blame the actor for what is the fault of the poet is to injure both. The actor loses heart, and the poet is made self-confident.

GOTTHOLD LESSING

If one or two actors in a production give bad performances, the actors are at fault. If all the performances are bad, it's the director's fault.

LEE STRASBERG

Any actress can play a bereaved mother. Playing a bereaved mother in a play which isn't serious is something else again.

ERIC BENTLEY

Today Hamlet, tomorrow a supernumerary, but even as a supernumerary you must become an artist.

KONSTANTIN STANISLAVSKY

ACT ONE
Scene Seven:
Acting in Companies...and Alone

To Stanislavsky the very idea of an actor who does not form part of a permanent company is inconceivable.

DAVID MAGARSHACK

Now, I really do make them play Hamlet one night and the butler the next. The gain is that you get a rested Hamlet. The butler is usually overdone.

PETER DAWS

In the small hours, every actor will tell you that he wants to join a company, and play Hamlet on Monday and the butler on Tuesday. The trouble is, there aren't enough Hamlets to go round.

PETER HALL

It is very hard to cast a number of plays adequately from the same company of actors without several parts being miscast.

JOHN GIELGUD

Actors frequently express a passionate desire to work in a rep theatre—no amount of effort would be too much, no amount of sacrifice would be too great. But when they are presented with a hard-and-fast proposition their enthusiasm all too often vanishes.

EVA LEGALLIENNE

Two actors spot each other while crossing the plains of Kansas. One is heading west to Los Angeles, the other east to New York. Simultaneously, they shout, "Go back!"

ANONYMOUS

The first great threat to the native repertory system lies in the inner nature of the American theatre artists. The repertory system demands the absolute submission of the individual to a high ideal; yet, the majority of our theatre eminences are primarily interested in the advancement of their own career.

ROBERT BRUSTEIN

Paula Kingsley: Think what we've come through! Tent shows, riverboats, rep companies—

Laurence Brooks: We had to do all that, darling, to be here tonight. It's been worth it.
Paula: Worth it? Why, it's our life, darling—it's acting, it's theatre! Even if we were still back in that rep company, or in a tent, or on the river—I wouldn't care. It's Theatre!

Backstage after the Broadway opening of *The Lady of the Rose*, in *The Fabulous Invalid* by Moss Hart and George S. Kaufman

The excitement occasioned by the presence of the London manager increased a thousand-fold. . . . Everybody who was on the stage beheld no audience but one individual; everybody played to the London manager. . . . At length the London manager was discovered to be asleep, and shortly after that he woke up and went away.

CHARLES DICKENS, on the hopes of the regional troupe in *Nicholas Nickleby*

The more the actor wishes to amuse his audience, the more the audience will sit back in comfort waiting to be amused.

KONSTANTIN STANISLAVSKY

You can pick out actors by the glazed look that comes into their eyes when the conversation wanders away from themselves.

MICHAEL WILDING

An actor's a guy who if you ain't talkin' about him, ain't listening.

MARLON BRANDO

Some of the greatest love affairs I've known have involved one actor, unassisted.

WILLIAM MIZNER

It is a great help for a man to be in love with himself. For an actor, however, it is absolutely essential.

ROBERT MORLEY

A fan club is a group of people who tell an actor he is not alone in the way he feels about himself.

JACK CARSON

Modesty in an actor is as fake as passion in a call girl.

JACKIE GLEASON

Eve Harrington: It's not modesty, I just don't try to kid myself.
Addison DeWitt: A revolutionary approach in the theatre.

In *All about Eve* by Joseph L. Mankiewicz

You can't steal enough money in a lifetime to make up for the psychological damage. . . . There's no question you get pumped up by the recognition, and then a kind of self-loathing sets in when you realize you're enjoying it.

GEORGE C. SCOTT

Sometimes I worry about being a success in a mediocre world.

LILY TOMLIN

Never say your salary is so-and-so; let them make you an offer first and then tell them, if necessary, what you had in your last engagement.

ELLEN TERRY, advising her nephew, John Gielgud

I had on my best suit and tried to look rather

113

arrogant, as I always do when money has to be discussed. "How nice to see you, dear," said Lilian [Baylis]. "Of course, we'd love to have you here, your dear aunt [Ellen Terry, former company member], you know—but of course we can't afford stars." By the end of the interview I was begging her to let me join the company.

JOHN GIELGUD, on becoming a member of the Old Vic

Nepotism runs through the theatre with the grandeur of the Mississippi at flood time.

MOSS HART

Life's what's important. Walking, houses, family. Birth and pain and joy. Acting's just waiting for a custard pie. That's all.

KATHARINE HEPBURN

Acting is not an important job in the scheme of things. Plumbing is.

SPENCER TRACY

And there is the fine story of the great Viennese actor Josef Kainz, who said he couldn't play Prospero because Prospero had to be a great man, and he wondered whether a great man would become only an actor.

HERBERT BLAU

We can telegraph and telephone and wire pictures across the ocean; we can fly over it. But the way to the human being next to us is still as far as the stars. The actor takes us on this way.

MAX REINHARDT

Drama is an art in which the actor serves the author and in which the other theatre artists serve the actor.

ERIC BENTLEY

A writer for the stage must face the fact that the making of a play is, finally, a collaborative venture, and plays have rarely achieved a full-scale success without being in some manner raised above their manuscript level by the brilliant gifts of actors, directors, designers, and frequently even the seasoned theatrical instincts of their producers.

TENNESSEE WILLIAMS

The poet, the actor, the artist, the tailor, the stagehand serve one goal, which is placed by the poet in the very basis of his play.

KONSTANTIN STANISLAVSKY

ACT ONE
Scene Eight:
Designing Ways

The sole aim of the arts of scene-designing, costuming, lighting, is to enhance the natural powers of the actor.

ROBERT EDMOND JONES

The truth is, that the spectators are always in their senses, and know, from the first act to the last, that the stage is only a stage, and that the players are only players.

SAMUEL JOHNSON

What child is there, that coming to a play, and seeing "Thebes" written in great letters upon an old door, doth believe that it is Thebes?

PHILIP SIDNEY

The aim of art is to represent not the outward appearance of things, but their inward significance.

ARISTOTLE

A stage set should not make a pretty picture of its own. The empty stage should look formal and pleasing, but should seem to be waiting for the action to complete it: it should not hold definite significance in itself.

G. WILSON KNIGHT

There is no more reason for a room on a stage to be a reproduction of an actual room than for an actor who plays the part of Napoleon to be Napoleon or for an actor who plays Death in the old morality play to be dead.

ROBERT EDMOND JONES

An original painter knows, of course, that when the public demands likeness to an object, it generally wants the exact opposite, likeness to the pictorial conventions it is familiar with.

NORTHROP FRYE

A play is a painting that moves. Instead of it holding still and you looking at it, you hold still and it scrolls by.

PATRICIA ZIPPRODT

Cubism was born from Harlequin's costume.

ERIC HELLER

One famous actor . . . said that when he was to act in one of his ordinary suits, he would take it off on arriving at the theatre and hang it up. . . . When his make-up was on and it was time for his entrance he would put it on again . . . . But it was no longer an ordinary suit, it was converted into the outer mantle of the character he was playing.

KONSTANTIN STANISLAVKSY

Why don't I just give you some money, then you can buy whatever you want to wear on stage. You obviously want a shopper, and I am merely a designer.

NAN CIBULA-JENKINS, to an uncooperative actress during a costume fitting

Next to a tenor, a wardrobe woman is the touchiest thing in show business.

BIRDIE, in *All about Eve* by Joseph L. Mankiewicz

119

There's hills in them thar gold.

ALFRED HITCHCOCK, upon seeing Tony Duquette's golden dress on Grace Kelley in *To Catch a Thief*

If a woman is poorly dressed you notice her dress. If she's impeccably dressed you notice the woman.

COCO CHANEL

All women's dresses, in every age and country, are merely variations on the eternal struggle between the admitted desire to dress and the unadmitted desire to undress.

LIN YUTANG

Every time a woman leaves off something she looks better, but every time a man leaves off something he looks worse.

WILL ROGERS

Clothes make the man. Naked people have little or no influence in society.

MARK TWAIN

A cloak for to go invisible.

PHILIP HENSLOWE, in his 1598 inventory, possibly referring to Puck's costume in *A Midsummer Night's Dream*

The stage in Shakespeare's time was a naked room with a blanket for a curtain; but he made it a field for monarchs.

SAMUEL TAYLOR COLERIDGE

Ruth Gordon (*describing a new play*): There's no scenery at all. In the first scene, I'm on the left side of the stage and the audience has to imagine I'm in a crowded restaurant. In Scene Two, I run over to the right side of the stage and the audience has to imagine I'm in my own drawing room.

George S. Kaufman: And the second night you'll have to imagine there's an audience out front.

Has anyone understood that the basic thing about Elizabethan theatre is that it was played in daylight? The actor saw the eyes of the audience.

PETER HALL

Shakespeare knew more than all of us. How he uses sunlight, moonlight, candlelight, torchlight, starlight.

ROBERT EDMOND JONES

Put out the light, and then put out the light.

OTHELLO, in the play by William Shakespeare

Lights are to drama what music is to the lyrics of a song. The greatest part of my success in the theatre I attribute to my feeling for colors, translated into effects of light.

DAVID BELASCO

If I am so insistent about the bright lights, both the stage and house lights, it is because I should in some way like both actors and audience to be caught up in the same illumination, and for there to be no place for them to hide, or even half-hide.

JEAN GENET

In a circle of light on the stage in the midst of darkness, you have the sensation of being entirely alone. . . . This is called solitude in public. . . . You can always enclose yourself in this circle, like a snail in its shell.

KONSTANTIN STANISLAVSKY

The property master of a Shakespeare production will find his task of collecting scenic, utility, and acting properties far from difficult.

J. C. ADAMS

I will obviate the need to carry around sets, props, and costumes.

AUGUST STRINDBERG

I can take any empty space and call it a bare stage. A man walks across this empty space whilst someone else is watching him, and this is all that is needed for an act of theatre to be engaged.

PETER BROOK

We're so proficient at creating illusion in the theatre that we often fool ourselves.

JOHN HIRSCH

I've listened backstage to people applaud. It's like waves of love coming over the footlights and wrapping you up. Imagine, to know every night that different hundreds of people love you. They smile, their eyes shine, you please them. They want you. You belong.

EVE HARRINGTON, in *All about Eve* by Joseph L. Mankiewicz

(*Curtain*)

124

ENTR'ACTE:
Backstage Whispers

The criticism that theatre people make of one another is usually of devastating severity—but absolutely precise.

    PETER BROOK

Sarah Bernhardt? A great actress—from the waist down.

    MADGE KENDAL

I saw the play at a disadvantage. The curtain was up.

    GEORGE S. KAUFMAN

Anyone with talent should leave at once.

    TYRONE GUTHRIE, concluding a consultation for Australia to establish a national theatre

No good deed goes unpunished.

    CLARE BOOTHE LUCE

The one thing constant in a changing world is the avant-garde.

LOUIS JOUVET

Experimentation must be rebellion. It reacts against an established object like Newton's law of motion. In that sense many of the changes in American experimental theatre may just be part of an organic evolution.

ROBERT MARX

He's one of those original thinkers in the theatre, the kind who never holds an opinion that isn't fashionable, who always shows the courage of other people's convictions.

ROCCO LANDESMAN

The theatre community is made up of what Howard Rosenberg once called "a herd of independent minds."

ROBERT BRUSTEIN

Invective is one of the most readable forms of literary art, just as panegyric is one of the dullest.

NORTHROP FRYE

I move that Euripides be taken care of in some permanent and unpleasant way: poison, perhaps, or a more sublime medium.

CHOREGUS, in *The Thesmophoriazusae* by Aristophanes

I portray men as they ought to be portrayed, but Euripides portrays them as they are.

SOPHOCLES

Your recent stuff's been pretty peculiar. What was *The Winter's Tale* about? I ask to be polite.

BEN JONSON, speaking to William Shakespeare in *Bingo* by Edward Bond

He hasn't an enemy in the world, and none of his friends like him.

OSCAR WILDE, on George Bernard Shaw

I cannot say that I greatly cared for *The Importance of Being Earnest*. It amused me, of course; but unless comedy touches me as well as amuses me, it leaves me with a sense of having wasted my evening.

GEORGE BERNARD SHAW

The first man to have cut a swath through the theatre and left it strewn with virgins.

FRANK HARRIS, on George Bernard Shaw

Frank Harris is not second-rate, nor third-rate nor fifth. He is just his own horrible self.

GEORGE BERNARD SHAW

Shaw writes like a Pakistani who has learned English when he was twelve years old in order to become a chartered accountant.

JOHN OSBORNE

Man's inhumanity to man
Makes countless thousands mourn!

ROBERT BURNS

130

Writers seldom wish other writers well.

SAUL BELLOW

Intellectuals are like the mafia. They only kill their own.

WOODY ALLEN

One of the most characteristic sounds of the English Sunday morning is the critic Harold Hobson barking up the wrong tree.

PENELOPE GILLIAT

I'm often astonished how some people whose whole life is devoted to an art form which in basic terms is meant to encourage human beings to behave better to each other and be more humane, can personally on occasion be such shits: public moralists and private shits.

PETER HALL

Nobody dislikes theatre as much as theatre practitioners do.

J. R. SULLIVAN

ACT TWO
Scene One:
Transforming Page to Stage

Rehearsing a play is making the words flesh.
Publishing a play is reversing the process.

 PETER SHAFFER

Watching my plays performed in London is
like seeing them in translation.

 LILLIAN HELLMAN

He's having all his books translated into French.
They lose something in the original.

 JAMES THURBER

Poetry is the thing that, when a poem is translated, gets left out.

 ROBERT FROST

Translation is not mainly the work of preserv-
ing the hearth—a necessary task performed by
scholarship—but of letting a fire burn in it.

 RICHARD EDER

To translate well is a difficult matter. It is not simply a question of rendering the meaning, but also, to a certain extent, of remodeling the expression and the metaphors, of accommodating the outward form to the structure and requirements of the language into which one is translating.

HENRIK IBSEN

"There! Just turn that into English, and put your name on the title page. Damne me," said Mr. Crummles angrily, "if I haven't often said that I wouldn't have a man or woman in my company that wasn't master of the language, so that they might learn it from the original, and play it in English, and by that means save all this trouble and expense."

NICHOLAS NICKLEBY receives his first translation assignment, in the novel by Charles Dickens

Whatever language I speak as the translator must either be the language of the audience, or, if it isn't their current language, be recognizable to them as an echo of what they already know. Theatre only works if the actors speak the same language as the audience. The language must be as natural in the actor's mouth as it is in the audience's ear.

PAUL SCHMIDT

It is far more essential to get good actors than a good play.

LEONE DI SOMI

I would take a bad script and a good director any day against a good script and a bad director.

BETTE DAVIS

Theatre consists of two great arts: acting and playwriting; and there is no third art necessary to coordinate them.

JAMES AGATE

Lee Richardson: How does one direct?
Tyrone Guthrie: You get some very good actors together who are foolish enough to trust you.

135

Theatre director: a person engaged by the management to conceal the fact that the players cannot act.

JAMES AGATE

The first quality that a [director] must have is an inability to act. Given that blockage to the expression of his/her personality, it naturally follows that if a person is still keen to impose something on the stage then they had better [direct]. Lack of talent is no bar.

MICHAEL GREEN

Finally, what is the theatre to the [director]? [Directors] come to the theatre after failing in other fields. He who once dreamed of becoming a playwright usually ends up as a [director]. The theatre critic who has long had an impotence complex towards an art which he can do no more than write about takes up [directing]. The hypersensitive professor of literature who is weary of academic work considers himself competent to become a [director]. He knows what drama is—and what else is theatre to him if not the realization of a text?

JERZY GROTOWSKI

The notes taken by the director as he silently watches the players are a test of his competence. If, for example, he writes: "the Oedipus Complex must be very apparent here, discuss with the Queen," the sooner he is packed out of the theatre and replaced, the better.

GEORGE BERNARD SHAW

If you write a line that you don't like, you can cross it out ferociously. You cannot do that to an actor or to a technician when they are offering their best.

EDWARD BOND

I don't believe you.

KONSTANTIN STANISLAVSKY, favorite acting note

The four worst words from a director in reply to a question I ask: "What do you think?"

JOHN MAHONEY

The best sort of performance, and by far the hardest to create, would make the play look as though it had [directed] itself.

G. WILSON KNIGHT

I think it is time there was an innovation to protect the author and the actor and the public from the vagaries of the director. Given a good play and a good team and a decent set you could put a blue-arsed baboon in the stalls and get what is known as a production.

PETER O'TOOLE

Speak the speech, I pray you, as I pronounced it to you, trippingly on the tongue; but if you mouth it, as many of your players do, I had as lief the town-crier spoke my lines. Nor do not saw the air too much with your hand, thus, but use all gently.

HAMLET, to the visiting troupe in the play by William Shakespeare

It takes a long while for a director to cease thinking in terms of the result he desires and instead concentrate on discovering the source of energy in the actor from which true impulses arise.

PETER BROOK

We both [Brook and I] feel that in a sense the concept of the director is moving away from the autocratic interpreter, the conductor who presents his view of the work, to someone who is much more like the trainer of a football team. The director trains and develops the group, but the group of course has to do the play, or play the match.

PETER HALL

The actor is an athlete of the heart.

ANTONIN ARTAUD

The greatest danger for a director is to yield to caprice.

VSEVOLOD MEYERHOLD

We have let the theatre become a director's fiefdom and in that lies some explanations of the decline of the playwright. Theatre art should precede the self (to paraphrase Stanislavsky), but as directors have assumed greater and greater authority, the playwright is diminished.

ARTHUR BALLET

The actors now count for more than the poets.

ARISTOTLE

The [director's] business is not translation but re-creation.

G. WILSON KNIGHT

Pinter's position is clear: an author has certain clear intentions, and Wilde's intentions [in *Earnest*] were not that the women should be played by men. Jonathan [Miller] asserted repeatedly that it was a director's right to reinterpret a play in any way that seemed significant to him, once the play was no longer new. He was making a fool of nobody but himself, and the play was still there at the end of the day. Harold feels one has a greater responsibil-

ity to a dead dramatist than to a living one.
  PETER HALL

I've never regarded myself as the one authority on my plays just because I wrote the damned things.
  HAROLD PINTER

A director is there to make visible what, without you, might perhaps never have been seen.
  ROBERT BRESSON

I believe that the great problem for the director is how to avoid imposing himself upon the play and the audience, and that his only safe course is to blank out from his mind any overall critical conceptions.
  ARTHUR HARBAGE

If you just let a play speak, it may not make a sound.
  PETER BROOK

There are no facts, only interpretations.
  FRIEDRICH NIETZSCHE

Interpretation is the revenge of the intellectual upon art.

SUSAN SONTAG

What one does on a first day [of rehearsal] is of little importance in itself; what matters is releasing tension, calming fears, and creating a climate in which confidence can develop.

PETER BROOK

But it always sounds terrible at a first reading. Didn't you know that? The second act will sound a little better, and by the third act they'll begin to forget themselves and even act it a little bit. You watch.

GEORGE S. KAUFMAN, to Moss Hart on a break at the first rehearsal of *Once in a Lifetime*

An actor hearing an author read a play in which he is to impersonate a character ought never to be told in advance the part which is to be assigned to him, as otherwise he only pays languid attention to everything that is not his part, and the ideas of the author escape him.

SARAH BERNHARDT

I speak, then some bullshit. I speak some more, more bullshit. Then I speak again.

ANONYMOUS ACTOR, describing his scene

If you can't keep a group of actors interested in rehearsal, you better get out of theatre.

TYRONE GUTHRIE

I found myself absolutely brimming with ideas, communicating easily with the actors, and the whole thing came to life very quickly. How can one explain these things? You do your prep, you sleep well, you think about it carefully, you are undistracted—and the rehearsal is like lead. You rush about like a flea in a fit, like I have today, and the work goes magnificently. It was worth being a director for those couple of hours.

PETER HALL

With no directorial vanity or ego of his own, he was able to indulge the actors in theirs, and an actor's ego in the early days of rehearsal is like a blade of new spring grass that will grow and reseed itself if it is not mowed down too quickly by a power-driven lawn mower—the lawn mower in most cases being the over-enthusiastic imposition of a famed directorial hand.

MOSS HART, on George S. Kaufman

"Don't [mark blocking in your script]. If I give you a bad move or suggest a bad move to you, you won't remember it. And that's a very good thing. We'll think of another one. If I give you a good move, you'll remember it." And I have never marked a move or anything else since, in a script. And he was right. When I have directed myself, I have always tried to persuade actors to do that.

ALEC GUINNESS, on rehearsing with Tyrone Guthrie

Go home, think about it, come back and astonish us in the morning.

TYRONE GUTHRIE, favorite note to actors at the end of a rehearsal

Astonish me.

SERGEI DIAGHILEV

Sometimes I had the feeling that he liked to put the stars downstage in the corner in the dark, while the extras were having a jolly good time picking their noses and scratching their bottoms, because he had a love of grotesque by-play which was very amusing and very lively.

JOHN GIELGUD, on Tyrone Guthrie

You've already shown me that—now show me something else.

HARLEY GRANVILLE-BARKER, to John Gielgud

And when I looked at my watch, we had been working on this short scene for forty minutes. It was extraordinary that he had the skill not to make you wild and not to exhaust you so much that you couldn't go on; if you had the strength to go along with him, he could give you more than any person I ever met in my life.

JOHN GIELGUD, on Harley Granville-Barker

In my experience tension and friction in rehearsal help no one—only calm, quiet, and great confidence can bring about the slightest glimmer of creativity.

PETER BROOK

I am a difficult actor and he is not an easy director. It makes a good combination. Easy actors and easy directors make mediocre art. Real art is a battle.

RYSZARD CIESLAK, on Peter Brook

Grotowski's actors offer their performance as a ceremony for those who wish to assist: the actor invokes, lays bare what lies in every man—and what daily life covers up.

PETER BROOK

Peter's greatest asset is that he is never satisfied.

YOSHI OIDA

I tried an exercise that Grotowski had invented. It seemed quite innocent: each person is invited to imitate the type of person he detests the most. "But there's a catch," said Grotowski.

"You will see. The actor will reveal his own deepest nature without knowing it."

PETER BROOK

Peter, we open in six days!

JOHN GIELGUD, answering Brook's rehearsal challenge that each actor do or say something shocking

Inspiration is nothing more complicated than knowing you have a deadline and will feel foolish if you don't meet it.

NORMAN COUSINS

The muses do not lead—they open the door and point at the tightrope.

JEAN COCTEAU

A director friend of mine who longed to be compared to Peter Brook once remarked: "I'd like to be a guru, but I can't do the silences."

DAVID HARE

He will change and change indefinitely, in search of rightness—and nothing is ever right.

PETER BROOK, on John Gielgud

I revered Gielgud as an artist and was totally glamorized by his personality, but he was a strict disciplinarian, intolerant of any slovenliness of speech and exasperated by youthful tentativeness. He was a living monument of impatience.

ALEC GUINNESS

He is inclined to despising the petty accessories of theatrical life which appeal so strongly to me—the gossip, the theatrical columns in the newspapers, the billing and the photographs in the front of the house.

JOHN GIELGUD, on Ralph Richardson

I was always rather amazed at him. A kind of brilliant butterfly while I was a very gloomy sort of boy.

RALPH RICHARDSON, on John Gielgud

The moment I read the play I saw Spooner clearly, which was rare for me. I remember saying to Harold Pinter, "I think Auden, don't you? Do you think sandals and socks?" and he jumped at the idea. Then I said, "Do you think we should add spectacles?" and he liked that too. About a week after we started rehearsal I came on the stage with a wig, the suit and the spectacles and everybody said, "It's exactly right, perfect!" And I said, "Yes, and now I must find a performance to go inside it!"

JOHN GIELGUD

I heard Ellen Terry sum up in a sentence this everlasting distinction between the actor's art and the playwright's. "My boy," she said to me, "act in your pauses." At those moments, you are a creator, not a servant of playwrights.

CEDRIC HARDWICKE

You've got to go from line to line, quickly and swiftly, never stop the flow of the lines, never stop. It's one joke after another, it's a firecracker. Always reserve the acting for underneath the spoken word. It's a musical play, a knockabout musical comedy.

GEORGE BERNARD SHAW, advising Ralph Richardson as Bluntschli and John Gielgud as Sergius in *Arms and the Man*

Laurence Olivier: Look, if you weren't so tall, I'd hit you. How can I love a part like Sergius, a stupid, idiot part? Absolutely nothing to do but to conform, to provide the cues for Shaw's ideas of what was funny at the time. How can you possible enjoy or like a part like that?
Tyrone Guthrie: Well, of course if you can't love him, you'll never be any good in him, will you?

All you can do with Shaw is to fan the actors out in a semicircle, put the speaker at the top, and hope for the best.

TYRONE GUTHRIE

Shaw is the only playwright on record to have deliberately withdrawn two of his early plays from production while still in rehearsal on the grounds that the actors weren't up to performing them properly.

JOHN F. MATTHEWS

The greatest guide to playing a dramatist is to listen to his tone of voice in ordinary life.

PETER HALL

Learn your lines, speak up, and don't fall over the furniture.

NOEL COWARD

You can't act words, and you can't act emotions, you can only act actions.

WILLIAM H. MACY

You must create a character that is entirely different from the character created by the author and when these two characters—the author's and the actor's—merge into one, you will get a work of art.

ANTON CHEKHOV

I beseech the theatres, the translators, the directors: take it, if you can use it, for your political fights, or whatever other fights you have. When you choose a play by me, change it, bring it totally onto the level of your society. Just don't make a display case! That's the most repugnant.

FRANZ XAVIER KROETZ

No changes of any kind may be made in the text of the play without prior written permission from Samuel French Inc. on behalf of the copyright owner. Unauthorized textual alterations constitute a violation of U.S. copyright law.

SAMUEL FRENCH INC., play-licensing agreement

Plays are not written, they are rewritten.

DION BOUCICAULT

Question: How many playwrights does it take to change a lightbulb?
Playwright: Change? Who said anything about change?

I always say I don't write with a hammer and chisel. It's just words on paper. Words are free. Start over and write something different. Explore that.

AUGUST WILSON

The players often mention it as an honor to Shakespeare that in his writing, whatsoever he penned, he never blotted out a line. My answer hath been, "Would he had blotted a thousand."

BEN JONSON

Reading Jonson is like wading through glue.

ALFRED, LORD TENNYSON

Read over your compositions and, when you meet a passage which you think is particularly fine, strike it out.

SAMUEL JOHNSON

Murder your darlings.

C. K. CHESTERTON

It is absolutely essential that all research of this kind be supervised by one or more theatre critics who, from the outside—rather like the Devil's Advocate—analyze the theatre's weaknesses and any alarming elements in the finished performances, basing their judgments on aesthetical principles identical to those of the theatre itself.

JERZY GROTOWSKI

Here's your play. The red markings are what you should cut, the pink markings are what doesn't work, and the blue markings need a total rewrite. And by the way, there's a big problem in your second act. I don't know what it is, but I'm not a playwright. Excuse me, I've got to get back to my translation of *Woyzeck Tonight*.

A. Rob "Beckett" Stern, "a promising young dramaturg," in *The Girl from Fargo: A Play* by Wendy Wasserstein and Terrence McNally

Whoever tries to stop me when I draw my sword is my enemy. His intention is of no concern.

ROBESPIERRE, in *Danton's Death* by Georg Büchner

I expect any day to pick up a matchbook cover with an advertisement for a "Correspondence School of Production Dramaturgy."

MARK BLY

There are three basic human drives: food, sex, and rewriting someone else's play.

ROMULUS LINNEY

A playwright's problem with premature suggestions can be that of a mother cat whose kittens have been handled too early. The ideas may be terrific, but they've got someone else's smell on them.

AMLIN GRAY

No passion in the world is equal to the passion to alter someone else's draft.

H. G. WELLS

Editing is the same thing as quarreling with writers—same thing exactly.

HAROLD ROSS

Editors are extremely fallible people, all of them. Don't put too much trust in them.

MAXWELL PERKINS

A dramaturg's job is not to get behind the wheel and drive the car away. Rather, our job is to point out to the driver/playwright the possible ways to fix the car himself.

ANNE CATTANEO

When I was writing *Rich and Famous*, I couldn't get the beginning right. Joe Papp said, "Go out there and tell the audience you don't have the beginning and these are the problems"— and it was hilarious.

JOHN GUARE

Shut up, Arnold, or I'll direct the play as you wrote it.

JOHN DEXTER, to Arnold Wesker during rehearsals of *Chicken Soup with Barley*

John Dexter, to whom I dedicate this book despite some things but because of most things.

ARNOLD WESKER

ACT TWO
Scene Two:
Encountering the Audience

The drama's laws, the drama's patrons give,
For we that live to please, must please to live.
SAMUEL JOHNSON

The [ancient Greek] audience was not primarily to be held by the factor of suspense or the desire to see what happens. And this was the most fitting condition for an art form which was to invite not a passing curiosity, but profound contemplation of eternal truths.
E. F. WATLING

We should return to the Greeks, play in the open air: the drama dies of stalls and boxes and evening dress, and people who come to digest their dinner.
ELEANORA DUSE

My plays make people uncomfortable because when they see them they have to think, and most people want to be effortlessly entertained, not to be told unpleasant truths. . . . People who are afraid of being alone with themselves, thinking about themselves, go to the theatre as they go to the beach or to parties—they go to be amused.

HENRIK IBSEN

Thinkers put some portion of an apparently stable world in peril, and no one can wholly predict what will emerge in its place.

JOHN DEWEY

The purpose of the theatrical enterprise should be to undermine the assumptions of middle-class institutions.

ANTON CHEKHOV

The nineteenth century saw the ascendancy of the middleclass, and as all the champions of genuine culture realized, this meant an ascendancy of the middle-class mind. It meant the apotheosis of mediocrity.

ERIC BENTLEY

There is only one sin in the arts—mediocrity.

MARTHA GRAHAM

It is so much worse to be a mediocre artist than to be a mediocre post office clerk.

RUDOLPH BING

Generally speaking, the American theatre is the aspirin of the middle classes.

WOLCOTT GIBBS

Art has become the after-dinner mint of the rich.

SAMUEL BARBER

The theatre is the only branch of art much cared for by people of wealth; like canasta, it does away with the bother of talk after dinner.

MARY MCCARTHY

No one ever went broke underestimating the intelligence of the public.

P. T. BARNUM

Never underestimate the ignorance of the American audience.

GEORGE JEAN NATHAN

An audience as a whole is sharper than any single member of it.

PETER HALL

Give an audience a chance, and it will certainly be wrong.

HERBERT BLAU

When the American public walks, its knuckles graze the ground.

GORE VIDAL

A nice respectable, middle-class, middle-aged maiden lady, with time on her hands and the money to help her pass it . . . let us call her Aunt Edna. . . . Aunt Edna is universal, and to those who feel that all the problems of the modern theatre might be saved by her liquidation, let me add that . . . she is also immortal.

TERENCE RATTIGAN

In America they criticize you if your ideas about a play are too radical. In Europe, they kill you if they aren't.

RICHARD SCHECHNER

In the theatre the audience wants to be surprised—but by things they expect.

TRISTRAM BERNARD

The artist will go on imitating without knowing what makes a thing good or bad, and may be expected therefore to imitate only that which pleases the taste or wins approval of the ignorant multitude.

PLATO

An artist is entitled to assume that his public is less interested and less sophisticated than himself in his particular field. He is not entitled to assume that his public is, in general, less intelligent or sensitive than himself; or that well-off, well-educated people are more intelligent and sensitive than others who have not enjoyed the same advantages.

TYRONE GUTHRIE

161

We beat ourselves up too much about audiences; the majority of people have always been drawn to popular entertainment. Most of Shakespeare's audience preferred bear-baiting.

ROBERT FALLS

I am a playwright who wants an audience of over-educated dilettantes and wannabe intellectuals—people like me, in other words.

TONY KUSHNER

I write plays for people who wouldn't be caught dead in the theatre.

BARRIE KEEFE

On the whole it is true that the younger an audience, the more swift and free its reactions. It is true that on the whole what alienates young people from the theatre is what is bad in theatre anyway, so in changing our forms to woo the young we would seem to be killing two birds with one stone.

PETER BROOK

It's hard for anybody young to realize why older people go to the theatre. Personally, I think it's because they've nothing else to do.

BERTOLT BRECHT

The tragedy of Brecht's life boils down to this simple fact: he gained the admiration and respect of those whom he professed to despise—the poets, the intellectuals, the West; and he failed to gain the one audience in the world for whom he claimed to write—the working class, the Party, the East.

ERNEST BORNEMANN

Hardly anybody listens in the theatre to anything he doesn't know already.

DENIS JOHNSTON

The alternative to pleasing an audience for two hours is to put the utmost strain upon their attention for three, and send them home exhausted but impressed.

GEORGE BERNARD SHAW

The artistic play and artistic imitation carried out by adults, which, unlike children's, are aimed at an audience, do not spare the spectators (for instance, in tragedy) the most painful experiences and can yet be felt by them as highly enjoyable.

SIGMUND FREUD

Now art should never try to be popular. The public should try to make itself artistic.

OSCAR WILDE

Samuel Beckett once confided to me that for him a play was a ship sinking not far from the coast while the audience watches helplessly from the cliffs as the gesticulating passengers drown.

PETER BROOK

While a theatre is a public art and belongs to its public, it is an art before it is public and so it belongs first to itself and its first service must be self-service.

ZELDA FICHANDLER

164

A repertory company can develop a great vision only if it is supported by an intelligent, imaginative, and enthusiastic audience, but the typical American theatre-goer of today is the most passive, immobile, and moribund spectator in the world.

ROBERT BRUSTEIN

The trouble with the theatre is that it's no longer a way of life for an audience. It's just a way to kill an evening.

JESSICA TANDY

If you want to help the American theatre, don't be an actress, be an audience.

TALLULAH BANKHEAD

Acting before an audience is like riding a terrific roller coaster.

GEORGE C. SCOTT

The actor has exertion without feeling, the audience feeling without exertion.

DENIS DIDEROT

It is mistaken naturalness for the actors to play to each other as if no third person were present.

JOHANN WOLFGANG VON GOETHE

The Chinese artist never acts as if there were a fourth wall besides the three surrounding him. He expresses his awareness of being watched. This immediately removes one of the European stage's characteristic illusions. The audience can no longer have the illusion of being the unseen spectator at an event which is really taking place.

BERTOLT BRECHT

You must never say it is a bad audience. It is your business to make it a good one.

ELLEN TERRY

The art of acting consists in keeping people from coughing.

RALPH RICHARDSON

Lead the audience by the nose to the thought.

LAURENCE OLIVIER

The audience is an unruly beast, to be tamed and kept firmly in its place.
ALEC GUINNESS

The only real teacher of acting is the audience.
GEORGE C. SCOTT

If you give the audience a chance they'll do half your acting for you.
KATHARINE HEPBURN

You're feeling it, you silly bitch. Your business is to make *them* feel it.
TYRONE GUTHRIE, to an actor during rehearsal

The tact of audacity consists in knowing how far one can afford to go too far.

JEAN COCTEAU

If you cried a little less, the audience would cry more.

EDITH EVANS, counseling John Gielgud

Michael Hordern: Do you have any advice on how to play King Lear?
John Gielgud: All I can tell you is to get a small Cordelia.

Crying, after all, is not the sole object of acting. If it were, my old Aunt Minne would be Duse.

ROBERT LEWIS

The important thing in acting is to be able to laugh and cry. If I have to cry, I think of my sex life. If I have to laugh, I think of my sex life.

GLENDA JACKSON

I'm beginning to think that it's easier to scare people than to make them laugh.

JIM MORRISON

Laughter is much more important than applause. Applause is almost a duty. Laughter is a reward.

CAROL CHANNING

I have known an actor very naturally proud of gaining a round of applause after a long speech within a scene, but had the action been truly holding its audience, applause would have been impossible.

G. WILSON KNIGHT

He who seeks only for applause from without has all his happiness in another's keeping.

OLIVER GOLDSMITH

Every now and then, when you're on stage, you hear the best sound a player can hear. It's a sound you can't get in movies or in television. It is the sound of a wonderful, deep silence that means you've hit them where they live.

SHELLEY WINTERS

169

The "talkies" in no way conflict with the theatre. Canned vegetables can never entirely take
the place of those picked fresh from the gar-
den. No matter how good the record of a voice,
it cannot supplant the living voice itself.

EVA LEGALLIENNE

I thanked him for being so courageous, being
so ready to take such risks the day before the
first night. He said that however hard one
rehearsed, and however precise the work, acting on any first night was going out on a
tightrope. One was quite inclined to fall off.
So one might just as well do a pirouette into
the bargain.

PETER HALL, on Ralph Richardson

The hallmark of a good actor is his attitude
toward change. Most actors make decisions in
the first stages of rehearsal, chart the shortest
distance between two points and then proceed
in a straight line. For these, the rehearsal is a
tunnel with light on one end and light on the
other, and a great stretch of darkness in the
middle. Another sort of actor retains the abil-

ity to rethink and reorganize his role through-out. He follows every lead and yields to every permutation, and isn't put off by detours and secondary routes. He may take longer but when he does, he brings a better-rounded result.

CHARLES MAROWITZ

I have never known a situation when an audience rejected a play at a preview and later, after much more work had been done on it, were persuaded into accepting it. The first preview is the one where you know beyond doubt if the play actually works or doesn't.

PETER HALL

Working on a production in previews is like tinkering with a mobile suspended by a thread: every time you fix one part, you throw another out of balance. Then you attend to *that* part and try to restore the balance. This process continues until you run out of previews. Then you open. Sometimes everything is in balance by then, usually it isn't.

JOHN HIRSCH

A long notes session with the cast. It was uphill work. They already have that rather pleased remoteness which actors achieve once they have been in front of an audience. The director, who used to be the center of their working life, is now an adviser on the sidelines, rather like a football trainer shouting helplessly . . . while the chaps get on with playing the game.

PETER HALL

My characters speak before they think—just like in real life.

NOEL COWARD, favorite note to actors

If the worst comes to the worst we can always tell him the truth.

BINKIE BEAUMONT, advising Peter Hall on handling a recalcitrant actor

Rehearsing a play with no opening date is like protracted necking with no possibility of an orgasm.

PETER HALL

ACT TWO
Scene Three:
Opening Nights...and Critics

Opening night: The night before the play is ready to open.

GEORGE JEAN NATHAN

Opening night . . . you will find a sizable number of people with severe respiratory infections who have, it appears, defied their doctors, torn aside oxygen tents, evaded the floor nurses at various hospitals, and courageously made their way to the theatre to enjoy the play—the Discreet Choker and the Straight Cougher.

MIKE NICHOLS

Opening night, if the show was a hit, Mr. Abbott would have a glass of wine, dance with his favorite chorus girl, and celebrate. If the show was a flop, he'd have his glass of wine, dance with his favorite chorus girl, and say, "Well, this time it didn't work."

JOHN KANDER

You have disgraced yourselves again.

WILLIAM BUTLER YEATS, to the rioting audience on the opening night of Sean O'Casey's *The Plough and the Stars*

I think that first nights should come near the end of a play's run—as indeed, they often do.

PETER USTINOV

The first night of a new play, agonizing though it must always be for the sensitive player, does at least arouse in a company of actors a feeling of unselfishness. They are drawn together in the service of the play, regardless of the recognition each may hope to gain by his individual performance.

JOHN GIELGUD

No critic has ever seen me act.

MRS. MINNIE MADDERN FISKE

Young Actor (*after reading bad reviews*): Well, Larry, you know what they say: "Don't pay attention to the critics. After all, what do they know!"

Laurence Olivier: True, my boy—and especially important to remember when the notices are good.

The actor who has made mistakes will get a beating, the one who hasn't will get a drink.

Epilogue, *The Casket* by Plautus, who had been born a slave

There is no . . . slave in Algiers but has a better life than the actor. A slave works all day, but he sleeps at night; he has only one or two masters to please, and when he does what he is commanded, he fulfills his duty.

AUGUSTIN DE ROJAS

An artist must elect to fight for freedom or for slavery. . . . I have made my choice. I had no alternative.

PAUL ROBESON

In the theatre, the actor is in total control. The director wasn't in the house last night, the designer wasn't there, the author's dead. It's just us and the audience.

IAN MCKELLEN

175

I am watching your performance from the rear of the house. Wish you were here.

GEORGE S. KAUFMAN, telegram sent backstage to William Gaxton during a performance of Kaufman's *Of Thee I Sing*

Because drama is written to be played, it both offers and requires a peculiarly immediate understanding.

FRANCIS FERGUSSON

Theatre, when it is boring, is boring with an intensity and pervasive power that the other arts cannot rival.

KENNETH TYNAN

We either yield ourself to a work of art or we do not. We are either capable of escaping our intellectual preoccupations or we are not. . . . The standard of values of a poet and his characters calls for sympathy, not logical analysis.

ALFRED HARBAGE

Works of art are made with the help of emo-

tion and it takes emotion to appreciate them
properly.

PAUL WEISS

I saw *Julius Caesar* and the new Pantomime
. . . . The mingled reality and mystery of the
whole show . . . were so dazzling, and opened
up such illimitable regions of delight, that
when I came out into the rainy street, at twelve
o'clock at night, I felt as if I had come from the
clouds, where I had been leading a romantic
life for ages, to a bawling, splashing, link-lighted,
umbrella-struggling, hackney-coach-jostling,
pattern-clinking, muddy, miserable world.

CHARLES DICKENS

There is not a single sentence uttered by
Shakespeare's Julius Caesar that is, I will not
say worthy of him, but worthy of an average
Tammany boss.

GEORGE BERNARD SHAW

When critics disagree, the artist is in accord
with himself.

OSCAR WILDE

One cannot criticize anything that one has not, at one time, also loved.

FRIEDRICH NIETZSCHE

When I asked a journalist. . . how they produced such remarkable critics I was told about a very clever and purposeful method used in Germany. They let a young critic write an article full of praise. . . . Anyone could blame. . . but it took a specialist to praise.

KONSTANTIN STANISLAVKSY

Praise is saltwater. Drink it and you become thirsty.

DAVID HARE

A good many inconveniences attend playgoing in any large city, but the greatest of them is usually the play itself.

KENNETH TYNAN

Dramatic criticism is, or should be, concerned solely with dramatic art even at the expense of bankrupting every theatre in the country.

GEORGE JEAN NATHAN

The standards of the theatre are so low that the talents of a critic of art are not called for.

ERIC BENTLEY

A dramatic critic is a person who surprises the playwright by informing him what he meant.

WILLIAM MIZNER

Tell me, when you are alone with Max Beerbohm, does he take off his face and reveal his mask?

OSCAR WILDE

I have known no man of genius who had not to pay, in some affliction or defect either physical or spiritual, for what the gods had given him.

MAX BEERBOHM

A critic is someone who knows the way but can't drive the car.

KENNETH TYNAN

179

Critics are like eunuchs in a harem: they know how it's done, they've seen it done every day, but they're unable to do it themselves.

BRENDAN BEHAN

To be quite frank, the critic ought to say: "Gentlemen, I am going to speak about myself apropos of Shakespeare, apropos of Racine, apropos of Goethe."

ANATOLE FRANCE

The most insipid, ridiculous play that I ever saw in my life.

SAMUEL PEPYS, on *A Midsummer Night's Dream*

It is a vulgar and barbarous drama, which would not be tolerated by the vilest populace of France, or Italy. . . . One would imagine this piece to be the work of a drunken savage.

VOLTAIRE, on *Hamlet*

A strange, horrible business, but I suppose good enough for Shakespeare's day.

QUEEN VICTORIA, on *King Lear*

I cannot help being of opinion that the plays of Shakespeare are less calculated for performance on a stage than those of almost any other dramatist whatsoever.

CHARLES LAMB

The play performed last night is "simple" enough in plan and purpose, but simple only in the sense of an open drain; of a loathsome sore unbandaged; of a dirty act done publicly.

CLEMENT SCOTT, on Henrik Ibsen's *Ghosts*

If you were to ask me what *Uncle Vanya* is about, I would say about as much as I can take.

ROBERT GARLAND

What all this means only Mr. Pinter knows, for as his characters speak in non-sequiturs, halfgibberish and lunatic ravings, they are unable to explain their actions, thoughts or feelings. If the author can forget Beckett, Ionesco and Simpson he may do much better next time.

MANCHESTER GUARDIAN, on *The Birthday Party*

Dear Sir: I would be obliged if you would kindly explain to me the meaning of your play, *The Birthday Party*. These are the points which I do not understand: 1. Who are the two men? 2. Where did Stanley come from? 3. Were they all supposed to be normal? You will appreciate that without the answers to my questions, I cannot fully understand your play.

Dear Madam: I would be obliged if you would kindly explain to me the meaning of your letter. These are the points which I do not understand: 1. Who are you? 2. Where do you come from? 3. Are you supposed to be normal? You will appreciate that without the answers to my questions, I cannot fully understand your letter.

HAROLD PINTER, "Letters to the Editor," *London Daily Mail*, 1967

John Gielgud: What is the Briggs/Spooner scene for at the beginning of Act II? What does it give the audience?

Harold Pinter: I'm afraid I cannot answer questions like that, John. My work is just what it is. I am sorry.

I've already written a play about two old ladies.

LILLIAN HELLMAN, after seeing John Gielgud and Ralph Richardson in David Storey's *Home*

Everyone who goes to the theatre has a right to his own opinion, but he doesn't have a right to have it taken seriously.

TYRONE GUTHRIE

Ever since the critic has existed, he has been the mark of the author's scorn. His trade seems to consist in a double impertinence—that of telling his betters what they should write, and his equals what they should like.

JOSEPH WOOD KRUTCH

Asking a working actor what he thinks about critics is like asking a lamp-post how it feels about dogs.

CHRISTOPHER HAMPTON

I learned my first lesson about criticism: that it may all be worthwhile, but only a tiny bit will be worthwhile for me.

DAVID HENRY HWANG

With good critics we often lose all sense of reading criticism and simply have a sense of reading. We are simply enjoying a kind of literature.

STANLEY KAUFFMANN

The mark of a good critic is that he tells his readers what is happening in the theatre of the day; the mark of the great critic is that he tells them what is not happening in the theatre.

KENNETH TYNAN

Whenever an actor tells me, as he invariably does, that he has not seen any notices of his performance, I always know that he has *The Saturday Review* in his pocket; but I respect the delicacy of an evasion which is as instinctive and involuntary as blushing.

GEORGE BERNARD SHAW

In the end, I am the severest critic of our work—not the press, not the Board, not even the audience who are the terminus of all we do and the reason for our strivings. I along with my comrades who are on the firing line with me, and whose taste, intelligence, feelings, skills and very bodies are judged "yes, no, maybe" every month or so.

ZELDA FICHANDLER

The paradox of the critics' position is that they completely control the serious drama which they hardly ever claim to understand, while no one very much cares what they say of light entertainment which they are quite at home with. Where they have competence they have no power, and vice versa.

ERIC BENTLEY

Only an auctioneer can be equally appreciative of all kinds of art.

OSCAR WILDE

ACT TWO
Scene Four:
Commercial Success

The rule in the art world is: you cater to the masses or you kowtow to the elite; you can't have both.

BEN HECHT

Anyone who remains on the level standing pays only one English penny: but if he wants to sit, he is let in at a further door, and there he gives another penny. If he desires to sit on a cushion in the most comfortable place of all, where he not only sees everything well, but can also be seen, then he gives yet another English penny at another door.

THOMAS PLATTER, 1599

We've got to do something about it. It's shocking for people to pay ten and fifteen dollars to go to the theatre.

JOHN W. CARLETON, Broadway producer in *The Fabulous Invalid* by Moss Hart and George S. Kaufman, 1938

I can spit out these rough-and-tumble dramas as a hen lays eggs. It's a degrading occupation, but more money has been made out of guano than out of poetry.

DION BOUCICAULT, after the premiere of *The Poor of New York*, 1857

A work that is both artistically and commercially successful is based on a misunderstanding.

JEAN-LUC GODDARD

In order to fully realize how bad a popular play can be, it is necessary to see it twice.

GEORGE BERNARD SHAW

A play should give you something to think about. When I see a play and understand it the first time, then I know it can't be much good.

T. S. ELIOT

Any work of art that can be understood is the work of journalism.

TRISTAN TZARA

Tales easily understood are not well told.

BAAL, in the play by Bertolt Brecht

I felt that the word "theatre" had been narrowed down to meaning a "current success," as if all literature were narrowed down to the current "best seller."

EVA LEGALLIENNE

A best seller is the gilded tomb of a mediocre talent.

LOGAN PEARSALL SMITH

Disparagers ask what [Grein's Independent Theatre] is independent of. . . . It is, of course, independent of commercial success. . . . The real history of the drama of the last ten years is not the history of the prosperous enterprises . . . but of the forlorn hopes . . . of the Impossibilists.

GEORGE BERNARD SHAW

Nothing in these days is more destructive of true theatrical art than the long run.

HERBERT BEERBOHM TREE

The long run is a part of modern technocracy, like the assembly line. It is stultifying and frustrating.

EVA LEGALLIENNE

Rehearsal called tomorrow. Take out the improvements.

GEORGE S. KAUFMAN, backstage notice during the long run of a show he directed

Kevin Spacey: How do you get up every night, eight or seven or six performances a week, and make sure that you're there?

Jack Lemmon: Almost every theatre has a loudspeaker in the dressing room. . . . What I do is at about five minutes to curtain time, I get on a chair, I get up to the loudspeaker and I turn it up a little. Now, there's no actors yet, but there's audience. . . . And that audience is first night, every night. . . . They've never seen it, for all intents and purposes. And about a minute or two later, I turn it up another notch. And then just before curtain time, I've got that thing up as loud as it will get. And I tell you, it'll goose you up. It'll really get the adrenaline going.

Long runs have their advantages, however. To begin with, they are necessary for an actor if he is to attract the notice of a large public.

JOHN GIELGUD

It is all too easy for those who work in a theatre to be disproportionately puffed up by success and cast down by failure; and, as a result, to pursue too eagerly a popularity which is ephemeral and often achieved at the cost of eventual reputation.

TYRONE GUTHRIE

When an understudy goes on, the first night you always rejoice. He is a hero. The second night, he is not as big a hero. The third night the feeling is, when is that son of a bitch coming back.

ROBERT WHITEHEAD

I earn my living as an artist. So do my siblings. I don't think you have to earn your income as an artist to be an artist. But if you are an artist, then artist is what you do, whether or not you're paid for doing it; it is what you do, not what you are.

TONY KUSHNER

You can make a killing in the theatre, but you can't make a living in the theatre.

ROBERT ANDERSON

Perhaps in compensation for our unequal income structure, the country's cultural posture has traditionally been egalitarian.

ROBERT BRUSTEIN

I look forward to an America which will reward achievement in the arts as we reward achievement in business or statecraft.

JOHN F. KENNEDY

Somehow, the scientists always seem to get the penthouse, while the arts and the humanities get the basement.

LYNDON JOHNSON

"Puritanism and Big Business" an astute foreign observer once entitled his analysis of the American culture.

W. McNeil Lowry

You can't create a Trappist Monastery on Forty-second Street.

John Hirsch

Any moron can make money, and in show business any cretin can make money. My considerations have never been financial. A flop in my head is a show or an experience I didn't care for. And a hit in my head is something I enjoyed doing very much. You'd be surprised how many of my flops have been hits and hits flops.

Alexander H. Cohen

There's a horse's ass for every light on Broadway.

David Merrick, on fellow producers

It was never enough for him to succeed. His competitors had to fail.

Alexander H. Cohen, on David Merrick

There's a lot of schadenfreude in this business and resentment of success.

ROCCO LANDESMAN

To behold suffering gives pleasure, but to cause another to suffer affords an even greater pleasure.

FRIEDRICH NIETZSCHE

Whenever a friend succeeds, a little something in me dies.

GORE VIDAL

[Broadway] is the only theatre in the world where every artist—by this, I mean designers, composers, lighting electricians, as well as actors—needs an agent for his personal protection.

PETER BROOK

No to those agents who tell their artists what to play.

GIAN CARLO MENOTTI

Question: How many agents does it take to screw in a lightbulb?
Agent: I'll get back to you.

Policeman: Sir, I'm sorry to inform you that your agent raped your wife, murdered her and the children, then burned down your house?
Actor: You mean he came to my house?

Alan Jay Lerner: How did you like the show?
Hollywood Agent: I don't know. I haven't read the reviews yet.

Let every eye negotiate for itself, and trust no agent.

CLAUDIO, in *Much Ado about Nothing* by William Shakespeare

The relation of the agent to the producer is the same as that of the knife to the throat.

ANONYMOUS

Artists dream. To be an artist is to dream like no one else dares to dream. Artists dream in the morning, they dream all day, and then they dream at night. And when artists dream, they dream of money.

HAROLD CLURMAN

Clifford Odets: There's nothing to write a play about in a country that is spiritually bankrupt.
Paul Rosenfeld: Why don't you write a play about the spiritual bankruptcy?
Odets: What, and have it run three weeks?

Market forces are very dangerous when applied to the arts. Ask Van Gogh. Ask Mozart.
PETER HALL

Let us ever remember that there is no class of actors who stand so much in need of a retiring fund as those who do not win the great prizes, but who are nevertheless an essential part of the theatrical system, and by consequence bear a part in contributing to our pleasure. We owe them a debt which we ought to pay.
CHARLES DICKENS, speaking at the first anniversary dinner of the General Theatrical Fund for aged, sick, and indigent actors

A nation that does not support its theatre is—if not dead—dying; just as a theatre that does not capture with laughter and tears the social and historical pulse, the drama of its people, the genuine color of the spiritual and natural landscape, has no right to call itself theatre, but only a place of amusement. The theatre has to impose itself on the public, and not the public on the theatre. The word "art" should be written everywhere, in the auditorium and in the dressing rooms, before the word "business"gets written there.

FEDERICO GARCÍA LORCA

When in history have community standards told us what quality is, or excellence, or value? Great thinkers throughout history, starting with Shakespeare, have scorned the whole notion of community standards.

ROBERT BRUSTEIN

Hain't we got all the fools in town on our side? And ain't that a big enough majority in any town?

HUCKLEBERRY FINN, in the novel by Mark Twain

The most dangerous enemy is not an individual. Not an oligarchy. Not even a vocal minority. No, the real enemy is you, all of you, the moral, solid majority.

DR. STOCKMAN, in *Enemy of the People* by Henrik Ibsen

What depresses me is that up to quite recently I have always believed popular art in all its manifestations in history was popular because it had merit—in some sense it was good. The public's own vitality saw to that. But now this isn't so any more. Market research provides the right product, the public is manipulated: 1984 has come.

PETER HALL

It is unquestionably true that the need for art is not created by economic conditions. But neither is the need for food created by economics. On the contrary, the need for food and warmth creates economics.

LEON TROTSKY

The soul is a very expensive thing to keep: It eats music and pictures and books and mountains and lakes and beautiful things to wear and nice people to be with. In this country you can't have them without lots of money; that is why our souls are so horribly starved.

ELLIE DUNN, in *Heartbreak House* by George Bernard Shaw

For genius like Shakespeare's is not born among laboring, uneducated, servile people. It was not born in England among the Saxons and the Britons. It is not born today among the working classes. How, then, could it have been born among women whose work began . . . almost before they were out of the nursery?

VIRGINIA WOOLF

I'll bet Shakespeare compromised himself a lot; anybody who's in the entertainment industry does to some extent.

GRAHAM GREENE

If you don't like my principle. . . I have others.

GROUCHO MARX

When is a repertoire theatre not a repertoire theatre? When it is a success.

HERBERT BEERBOHM TREE

198

ACT TWO
Scene Five:
Resident Theatres

I have never understood why we should be the
only country in the so-called civilized world
that fails to recognize the need for another
kind of theatre, one that in no way competes
with or impinges upon the field of commercial
entertainment.

> EVA LEGALLIENNE, founder, Civic Repertory
> Theatre (New York, 1926) and American Repertory
> Company (New York, 1946)

The organization has the temerity to believe—
particularly in a time of economic stress—
that its aims should be a matter of real public
concern.

> HAROLD CLURMAN, co-founder, Group Theatre
> (New York, 1931)

This is a non-commercial theatre. It's got to be
run by a person who sees right from the start
that the profits won't be money profits.

> HARRY HOPKINS, on the idea of a Federal Theatre
> Project, 1934

I didn't head the Federal Theatre thing when President Roosevelt asked me to because I didn't agree with it. I felt it was encouraging mediocre theatre at best.

EVA LEGALLIENNE

This is an American job, not just a New York job. I want someone who knows and cares about other parts of the country. It's a job just down your alley.

HARRY HOPKINS, to Hallie Flanagan on her leading the Federal Theatre Project

Would we produce a play written by a Communist? If it was a good play, we would produce a play written by a Republican.

HALLIE FLANAGAN

They [players] are the abstract and brief chronicles of the time. After your death you were better have a bad epitaph than their ill report while you live.

HAMLET, in the play by William Shakespeare

This singles out a special group of professional people for a denial of work in their profession. It is discrimination of the worst type.

FRANKLIN D. ROOSEVELT, on the decision by Congress to stop funding the Federal Theatre Project

Art in America had hitherto been apart from politics; but these projects were at the core of life. If they were mixed up with politics, it was because life in our country is mixed up with politics.

HALLIE FLANAGAN

I want to be part of a civilization which is constantly being enriched. I like living in the age of the airplane and television, and I want to live in an age when there is great theatre everywhere.

MARGO JONES, founder, Theatre '47 (Dallas, 1947)

It's a beginning. Do you want a new theatre for Houston? Meeting 3617 Main. Bring a friend. Tuesday, October 7, 8:00 p.m.

NINA VANCE, text of the 214 postcards that helped her found the Alley Theatre (Houston, 1947)

Once we made the choice to produce our plays not to recoup an investment but to recoup some corner of the universe for our understanding and enlargement, we entered the same world as the university, the museum, the church, and became, like them, an instrument of civilization.

ZELDA FICHANDLER, co-founder, Arena Stage (Washington, D.C., 1950)

What we want is a truthful, nonviolent, anarchist revolution, and in a certain sense all of our work over the years has been to encourage people to create a better world.

JUDITH MALINA, co-founder, Living Theatre (New York, 1951)

I have always wanted to provide access to the best human endeavor to the greatest number of people. I believe that great art is for everyone—not just the rich or the middle class.

JOSEPH PAPP, founder, Shakespeare Festival/Public Theatre (New York, 1954)

It is astonishing, when you come to think of it, that most of the resident theatres were founded by people whom nobody ever heard of.

JULIUS NOVICK

In particular this theatre will strive to perfect the idiom, the invention, the creativity of the American Negro in the drama, dance and song. It shall simultaneously draw upon world culture to enrich this bounty. It shall be bound by *no* orthodoxy in this regard—and no beholden posture to the commercial theatre of its time, nor to the idle, impotent and obscurantist efforts of a mistaken avant-garde.

LORRAINE HANSBERRY, 1962 prospectus for the John Brown Memorial Theatre of Harlem, never founded

It is all too easy for the audience of a theatre to take an irresponsible view of its share in the creation of standards; to assume that "support" is enough, without regard to the quality of the support. That attitude belongs to an era when the theatre was organized as a business and the

public had no more responsibility than a pur-
chaser of merchandise. Those days are ending.

TYRONE GUTHRIE, co-founder, Stratford National
Theatre (Ontario, 1953) and Minnesota Theatre
Company (Minneapolis, 1963)

This is an extremely foolish and stupid and
idiotic kind of attitude—to expect theatres to
make money. Do the public schools make
money? Do libraries make money? Does the
zoo make money? Do the sewers make money?
It's a community service.

JOHN HIRSCH, co-founder, Manitoba Theatre
Company (Winnipeg, 1958)

How do you teach someone that a theatre
comes about first as an idea, from an individual who has a philosophy and a passion? That
a theatre's idea is its heart and individual soul?
That the person who creates it must have the
desire not only to create work, but also to create the conditions in which that work can
live—and in which others can do it as well?
How do you teach someone to want to be a
midwife as well as a mother?

ROBERT KALFIN, founder Chelsea Theatre (New
York, 1965)

We challenge Chicanos to become involved in the art, the lifestyle, the political and religious act of doing theatre.

LUIS VALDEZ, founder, El Teatro Campesino (California, 1965)

Everyone involved with the commercial theatre is under the obligation to make money for his or her investors and for himself or herself. When that is your animating motive, then all decisions are made accordingly. . . . The alternative—in which your animating motive is to create a work of art, a collective work of art— is a socialist idea, not a capitalist idea. And it's very hard for a socialist idea to survive in an essentially ravenous capitalist society.

ROBERT BRUSTEIN, founder, Yale Repertory Theatre (New Haven, 1966) and American Repertory Theatre (Cambridge, 1979)

Someone once said that being an artistic director is the intelligent exercise of one's own taste. And that is what I believe with all my heart and soul. If you start second-guessing yourself in advance, I think you're done for.

ANDRE BISHOP

The artistic director gratifies his special need to relate to people in a highly accentuated paternalistic and maternalistic fashion.

PHILIP WEISSMAN

I felt I would take the lesser role in the theatre of administrator and director. It is a lesser role because the main figure in the theatre is the actor.

JOSEPH PAPP

An institution is the lengthened shadow of one man.

RALPH WALDO EMERSON

Most [artistic directors] are even less committed to a particular kind of play or style of playing than to a particular locality.

JULIUS NOVICK

Geography is destiny.

GARLAND WRIGHT

I'm leaving. Now they have to run the place. That's enough revenge for me.

ALVIN EPSTEIN, after the board of the Guthrie Theater terminated his contract as artistic director

What got you here will get you out of here.

JOE GARAGIOLA

There are only three things you can do in a difficult situation. You can leave it, you can change it, or you can die in it.

HENRIK IBSEN

If a particular public wants to have a serious theatre it must undertake the responsibility not merely of a customer but of a patron. That involves the exercise of taste.

TYRONE GUTHRIE

The ability of non-profit theatres to attain artistic and economic continuity as permanent institutions still remains to be demonstrated.

FORD FOUNDATION, *Annual Report*, 1964

Non-profit performing arts organizations should not be expected to pay their way at the box office. Indeed they cannot do so and still fulfill their true cultural mission.

ROCKEFELLER PANEL REPORT, *The Performing Arts: Problems and Prospects*, 1965

What we now have is probably better than what we had ten years ago.

RICHARD SCHECHNER, 1965

Hinterland Legits Top B'way.

VARIETY, 1966 headline

The regional theatre is stronger and more creative than ever before.

ARTHUR BALLET, 1973

Opportunities for artists have increased immeasurably; playwrights, directors and actors have widespread access to theatres committed to producing new work, and designers can expect to work with staffs capable of executing sophisticated and demanding productions in many theatre shops. The repertoires listed point out opportunities for artists that simply did not exist twenty-five years ago.

PETER ZEISLER, 1986

To be so preoccupied with vitality is a symptom of anemia.

GEORGE SANTAYANA

I have a hard time being told that this is just one of six plays and that the real product being provided is the season, that the individual play within the season is not the final product. It's not a very creative situation. As much as people berate Broadway producers, my experience on Broadway has been that this is the product and every effort is made to make it work. I find that very exciting.

MICHAEL MERRITT

I've never quite understood the idea of a "season." Whenever an artistic director says to me, "I have this slot," I always start to feel we're parking cars or something.

DAVID HENRY HWANG

209

ACT TWO
Scene Six:
Raising Money and Leading Theatres

I foresaw almost everything about the Festival. I was prepared for all kinds of struggles. The one thing I was not prepared for was the humiliating quest for money.

GIAN CARLO MENOTTI, on founding the Spoleto Festival USA

I have learned that if you have a million-dollar idea, you can raise a million dollars.

MARGO JONES

Make no small plans; they have no magic to stir men's blood and probably will not be realized.

DANIEL BURNHAM

The great giants of industry, banking and commerce can't get it through their heads that the more successful a repertory theatre is, the more it must cost. It contradicts all business principles.

ARTHUR MILLER

210

Many directors of corporate foundations and some university trustees handle money for research and education not as if they were engaged in a nonprofit enterprise, but as if they were engaged in an enterprise that was failing to make a profit. In other words, they do not see where the actual profit lies. It being intellectual and they not, it is to them invisible.

JACQUES BARZUN

Permanent deficit spending is publicly offensive to the foundations for the same reason that a national debt disturbs Senator Dirksen. It is not in the American tradition "to run a business that way."

RICHARD SCHECHNER

Civil servants, treasury officials and cabinet ministers still believe one should work in the arts for honor.

PETER HALL

Whether I was talking to an individual or to a foundation executive, my attitude was: nobody's doing me a favor by giving my theatre

money. "You're set up to give money!" I
would say to foundation executives: "You don't
have to give your money to me, but let's understand each other. You can't exist without people like me. You are mandated by law to spend
your money, and I'm giving you an opportunity to put it into something very important."
JOSEPH PAPP

Rapidly I discovered that seeking out private
sponsors was a dreary way of life, for apart
from the cocktails and the dinner parties, it
involved admiring wealthy people's collections
of paintings and sculpture and enduring long
gossip-filled phone calls that were mere wastes
of time. So I learned the much more agreeable
rules of begging from foundations, and I found
within them a serious and courteous form of
artistic patronage that resembled academic life.
PETER BROOK

Isn't giving money to New Dramatists like
helping people into hell?
WILLIAM INGE

No to fund-raising dinners, where rich people, in return for their money, are fed tepid chicken à la king, California wine, boring speeches and noncommittal conversation.

GIAN CARLO MENOTTI

The truly creative mind is hardly ever so much alone as when it is trying to be sociable.

RICHARD HOFSTADTER

Speaking of art... my husband can spit over a freight car.

MRS. POTTER PALMER

An artist should be fit for the best society and keep out of it.

JOHN RUSKIN

Board members believe that if the artists would just learn what the audience wants and give it to them, they would sell more tickets and raise more money. Organizations continually place people in positions with the expectation that they will meet unrealistic goals.

Consequently, they are given absolutely no chance of being successful.

NELLO MCDANIEL and GEORGE THORN

The familiar [funding] switchback. I shall once more be asked to cut according to my cloth, while others feel bound to criticize the style of the coat.

PETER HALL

No to those boards of directors and foundations that, because they furnish the money, want to impose with it their aesthetic judgment.

GIAN CARLO MENOTTI

The governors were hard put to it to persuade Lilian Baylis that such a pornographic piece was suitable to enliven the boards of her famous, but strictly moral, theatre.

JOHN GIELGUD, on the 1963 conflict within the Old Vic over producing William Congreve's *The Country Wife*, written in 1674

Among those who set themselves up as "agents of change," as philanthropists, as people of ethical credibility and ethical vision, there can

214

be no shortage of vanity and conceit, of cruelty and selfishness, of lies and deception.

ANNA FREUD

All's fair in love and business.

ROLAND LIEBER, Northlight Theatre trustee

If we can't raise questions of ethics and aesthetics with you, we might as well go out and raise money for the American Cancer Society, where everybody agrees that it's a good thing to cure cancer.

CHLOE OLDENBERG, Cleveland Play House trustee

All service is directly or indirectly ethical activity, a reply to a moral call within, one that answers a moral need in the world.

ROBERT COLES

How can you convince a board of directors that, by building bigger and worse opera houses, rich in bathrooms and restaurants but poor in acoustics and as intimate as air terminals, they actually endanger the future of opera?

GIAN CARLO MENOTTI

The contributions of a thriving cultural life to increasing tourist and convention business, attracting new industry, recruiting personnel—particularly when professional people are being transferred to a new location—also need to be stressed.

ROCKEFELLER FOUNDATION

I'm not sure how the Parthenon got built, or the Acropolis, but certainly it had nothing to do with revitalizing the neighborhood.

ALAN SCHNEIDER

Building concentrated arts centers in a single geographical location, we lend aid and comfort to the colonialist enclave theory—defending the last bastion of Western civilization against a hostile native population.

JOSEPH PAPP

I clawed this theatre out of the ground.

NINA VANCE

If a farmer fills his barn with grain, he gets mice; if he leaves it empty, he gets actors.

BILL VAUGHAN

216

The reason we can no longer build Gothic structures is because they were built from convictions, and we have only opinions.

HEINRICH HEINE

It's easier to allocate funds for buildings than for ideas.

PETER ZEISLER

Arnold Goodman pointed out that history is full of instances of foolish Boards and Committees and Proprietors suing architects or arraigning great artists, but history is always on the side of the artist.

PETER HALL

I think that the three of us have come as near to complete nervous breakdown as I have ever seen people verge on—not because of overwork, or hard work, but because of mental worry and strain. Personally, I do not wish to continue it.

LEE STRASBERG, to Cheryl Crawford and Harold Clurman, resigning as co-leader of the Group Theatre

It's splendid what you are doing at Stratford, but can I give you a word of advice? The day you feel that the walls are coming in on you, get out. No matter what the price or the difficulty. Get out.

GEORGE DEVINE, co-founder of the English Stage Company at the Royal Court, advising Peter Hall in 1961, five years before Devine died

Institutions have their place, but in my book they don't have much to do with living art. (Preservation and conservation are different matters.) They also exact a dreadful toll. To maintain an institution—which is what the [Royal] Court had become—before there was the state support which there is today . . . was the most killing job in the world.

TONY RICHARDSON

And yet I am at breaking point: very near the abyss which is all too familiar from Stratford days—an abyss which everybody faces who manages a theatre and tries as well to be an artist.

PETER HALL

The Court exacted its own loyalties even when they were already sadly academic. The fight went on, but out of duty, not vision. Duty finally kills. After our attempt at the Queen's season, the Court withdrew into what it has become ever since—a minor liberal institution with good intentions. That's why Konstantin shot himself.

TONY RICHARDSON

She loves the Theatre, she thinks she's serving the cause of humanity, she thinks she's a high priestess of Art, but what I think is, that kind of theatre is tired, it's all worn out.

KONSTANTIN, in *The Seagull* by Anton Chekhov

Suicide: a permanent solution to a temporary problem.

ANONYMOUS

If in the first act you hang a pistol on the wall, then in the last act it must be shot off. Otherwise you do not hang it there.

ANTON CHEKHOV

219

After my first acquaintance with Chekhov's *Seagull* I did not understand the essence, the aroma, the beauty of his play. . . . Nemirovich-Danchenko and I approached the hidden riches each in his own way, Vladimir Ivanovich by the literary road and I by the road of the actor, the road of images. Vladimir Ivanovich spoke of the feelings which he sought or foresaw in the play and the roles. I could not speak of them and preferred to illustrate them.

KONSTANTIN STANISLAVSKY

It came down to this: Stanislavksy had the last word in the region of form, and I in the region of content.

VLADIMIR NEMIROVICH-DANCHENKO

Nemirovich-Danchenko was forced to yield me the right of veto in matters of stage direction and artistic production. In the minutes I entered: The literary veto belongs to Nemirovich-Danchenko, the artistic veto to Stanislavsky.

KONSTANTIN STANISLAVSKY

Any repertoire is a house of cards. Pull one production away and the whole thing collapses.

PETER HALL

The production of classics is healthy, but . . . the seed of progress in the theatre lies in new plays.

MARGO JONES

What's a classic? Something that everybody wants to have read and nobody wants to read.

MARK TWAIN

When both the management and the audience know better what we can and ought to attempt, and also what we can and ought to afford, then we may take the risk of producing, and even commissioning, new work.

TYRONE GUTHRIE

The public is ahead of our ability to keep up with its taste. I'm less scared to give 'em what I didn't think they'd buy.

NINA VANCE

Complaints were centered not only on the season just past but on the one before it as well—the year when I had finally decided the theatre had an audience and could begin to close in on the kind of rep that really interested it. There had already been the long, patient years—hopefully unpatronizing—of spice and variety in between the pieces of meat: the Program for the Education, Pacification, and Diversification of the Audience.

ZELDA FICHANDLER

No David Merrick is more responsive to audience wishes than a producer who knows that his livelihood depends upon subscriptions.

RICHARD SCHECHNER

No terrible compromises. Just ones of "quiet desperation." The result? Subscriptions up, audience happy, seats filled, no strain, another day, another dollar.

ZELDA FICHANDLER

I, for one, cannot rally 'round a program which veers from British veterans . . . to modern Polish farce, culminating in a pseudo-psychic, quasi-crazy, ultra-umbilical entertainment, which has occupied the theatre for many months because it is popular. That seems to me to be nothing but a policy of commercial expediency and no more worthy of disinterested support than General Motors.

TYRONE GUTHRIE, ending his support of the Phoenix Theatre

In the end, the errors of pure art and of commercialized art are identical: they both appeal primarily to the senses. True art, on the other hand, is not merely a matter of pleasure.

ERIC BENTLEY

There are worrying signs that non-profit theatres moving into Broadway productions may risk losing artistic control of repertoire. It is very difficult to be just half commercial.

W. McNEIL LOWRY

There's no business like show business.

IRVING BERLIN

223

There's no profit like non-profit.

GERALD SCHOENFELD, chairman, The Shubert Organization

Pleasing the customers, giving them what they want in the form they expect, works for Coca-Cola—and it works for subsidized theatres, too. . . . The forces of the marketplace through the years have been just as effective a censor as government edicts.

ROCCO LANDESMAN, president, Jujamcyn Theaters

There is only one way to create a real theatre: to strive unbendingly to attract the devoted adherents as opposed to the transient public interested only in the hits.

JEAN-LOUIS BARRAULT

A good meeting with the Board. They asked tough questions; so did I. I told them that if I wanted to do a play I regarded as controversial, in any sense of the word, I would warn them about it and discuss it with them. If they wanted, they could of course read it. I appreciated that they had the right to overrule my decision and stop me doing such a play. But I wanted them to understand that if they did it twice, I would resign.

PETER HALL, before agreeing to succeed Laurence Olivier as head of the National Theatre

The history of these theatres illustrates a basic dilemma: In order to maintain freedom, it is necessary to remain small and modest; in order to improve production standards, it is necessary to expand. The more modest a theatre remains, the less able it is to improve its work; the more it expands, the less free it is to do what it wants.

JACK POGGI

It is the destiny of the theatre nearly everywhere and in every period to struggle even when it is flourishing.

HOWARD TAUBMAN

If politics is the art of the possible, theatre is the art of the impossible.

HERBERT BLAU

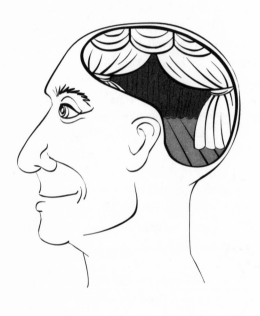

EPILOGUE:
The Fabulous Invalid Endures

Like most people I am a pessimist by experience, but an optimist by nature, and I have no doubt that I shall go on being true to my nature.

EDWARD BOND

A literature of despair is a contradiction in terms.

ALBERT CAMUS

The act of writing is an act of optimism. You would not take the trouble to do it if you felt that it didn't matter.

EDWARD ALBEE

My working definition of an optimist is a person who hasn't lived very long.

DORIS GRUMBACH

The theatre is always in trouble because its success depends upon too rare a set of coincidences.

ERIC BENTLEY

The city needs its playwrights.

ARISTOPHANES

To be an artist is to fail as no other dare fail.

SAMUEL BECKETT

Despair is normal in our work, it's the nature of the beastliness.

ALAN SCHNEIDER

No artist worthy of the name can escape the compulsive search for that platonic perfection, the elusiveness of which is its very essence, and therefore, avoid the bitterness of frustration. At best an artist can find a certain kind of serenity in resigning himself to the curse of imperfection.

GIAN CARLO MENOTTI

Starting from the hope that perhaps everything can be achieved in the theatre, we have
of course arrived at the conclusion that not so
terribly much has been achieved.

PETER STEIN

The theatre is always dying and always being
reborn, phoenix-like, at the very moment
when we have finished conducting the funeral
services over its ashes.

ROBERT EDMOND JONES

It's always a battle, the theatre. Every play.
Why, nothing could have been worse than the
opening night of *Hamlet*. You wouldn't have
given a tinker's dam for it.

WILLIAM SHAKESPEARE, in *The Fabulous Invalid* by
Moss Hart and George S. Kaufman

We tend to forget that even in great eras,
genius has been rare. I prefer art, but I'll settle
for less.

HAROLD CLURMAN

So many things in the theatre are discouraging
that any man of sense would give it up. But the
theatre is a femme fatale, and for those who
feel her fascination, the question: What is to
be done? has perpetually to be asked and perpetually to be answering affirmatively.

ERIC BENTLEY

It is not within thy power to finish the task nor
is it thy liberty to abandon it.

ANCIENT SAGE, in *The Convict's Return* by Geoff
Hoyle

Art is always in crisis: you must work fast
To write in the breath on the window.

EDWARD BOND

The stage is life, music, beautiful girls, legs,
breasts, not talk or intellectualism or dried-up
academics.

HAROLD CLURMAN

Listen, junior, and learn. You want to know
what the theatre is? A flea circus. Also opera.
Also rodeos, carnivals, ballets, Indian tribal

dances, Punch and Judy, a one-man band—all theatre. Wherever there's magic and make-believe and an audience there's theatre. Donald Duck, Ibsen and the Lone Ranger, Sarah Bernhardt and Poodles Hanneford, Lunt and Fontanne, Betty Grable, Rex the Wild Horse, Eleanora Duse—all theatre. You don't understand them. You don't like them all. Why should you? The theatre's for everybody—you included, but not exclusively. So don't approve or disapprove. It may not be *your* theatre, but it's theatre for somebody, somewhere.

BILL SIMPSON, in *All About Eve* by Joseph L. Mankiewicz

The grubby rewards the theatre offers, except to the privileged few, make it hard to understand the undaunted loyalty it calls forth or the passion with which it is pursued.

MOSS HART

The supreme accomplishment is to blur the line between work and play.

ARNOLD TOYNBEE

Play may be taken seriously, but it is the play and not ourselves that we are taking seriously or else it is not really play at all.
ELLEN LANGER

All's well that ends.
SAMUEL BECKETT

How you spend your days is how you spend your life.
ANNIE DILLARD

There is only one success—to spend your life in your own way.
CHRISTOPHER MORLEY

And now the play is played out, and of rhetoric enough.
SOCRATES

(*Exeunt Omnes*)